Got it! PLUS

Level 2

Student Book & Workbook

with Online Skills Practice

Philippa Bowen & Denis Delaney

OXFORD
UNIVERSITY PRESS

Contents

Unit	Vocabulary	Grammar
Welcome page 4	Physical descriptions Music Jobs Movies Transportation Food and drink Geography Feelings and emotions	Simple present / Present progressive *be*: Simple past Simple past Present progressive for future *How long ...? + take* some / any with countable / uncountable nouns *a lot of / much / many / a little / a few* Comparative adjectives Superlative adjectives
1 Nobody lives here page 10	Places around town	*must* (affirmative and negative) Compounds: *some / any / no* Compounds: *every*
2 I have to clean my room page 18	Housework	*have to* (affirmative, negative, interrogative, and short answers) *mustn't / don't have to* Gerunds Verb + *-ing* form
Review A: pages 26–27	**Culture club A: page 28**	**My progress A: page 29**
3 What are you going to do? page 30	Personality	*be going to* (1) (affirmative, negative, interrogative, and short answers) *be going to* (2) Verb + infinitive / *-ing* form
4 What will it be like? page 38	The weather	*will*: future (affirmative, negative, interrogative, and short answers *will / be going to* First conditional
Review B: pages 46–47	**Culture club B: page 48**	**My progress B: page 49**
Remember: pages 50–51		
5 I've done that! page 52	Exciting experiences	Present perfect (affirmative and negative) Past participles *been / gone* Present perfect (interrogative and short answers) *ever / never* Present perfect / Simple past
6 I haven't finished it yet page 60	Books	Present perfect + *yet* and *already* Present perfect + *just* Present perfect + *for / since*
Review C: pages 68–69	**Culture club C: page 70**	**My progress C: page 71**
7 What were they doing? page 72	Crime	Past progressive (affirmative, negative, interrogative, and short answers) *while* Past progressive and Simple past + *when / while*
8 I use the Internet to chat page 80	Human achievement	Relative pronouns: *who / which / that* The infinitive of purpose *Which one ...? / Which ones ...?*
Review D: pages 88–89	**Culture club D: page 90**	**My progress D: page 91**
Wordlist: pages V1–V3		
Workbook: pages W1–W49		

Communication	Skills
Asking for and giving directions **Pronunciation:** /r/	**Reading:** A magazine article about online safety **Listening:** A police officer talking about road safety **Speaking:** Road safety rules **Writing:** A text about road safety rules
Asking for permission **Pronunciation:** *have* /hæv/ and *have to* /hæf tə/	**Reading:** A magazine article about active teenagers **Listening:** A radio show about lazy teenagers **Speaking:** Asking and answering questions about housework **Writing:** A text about your weekly schedule
Curriculum extra A, Chemistry: pages C1–C2	
Inviting people to do things **Pronunciation:** Rising and falling intonation	**Reading:** A magazine article about star signs **Listening:** A conversation about star signs **Speaking:** Future plans **Writing:** An e-mail about future plans
Making offers **Pronunciation:** *'ll*	**Reading:** A magazine article about the environment **Listening:** A conversation about the environment **Speaking:** Calculating your carbon footprint **Writing:** A description of your carbon footprint
Curriculum extra B, Physics: pages C3–C4	
Booking an activity **Pronunciation:** Strong and weak forms of *have*	**Reading:** A magazine article about a family traveling around the world **Listening:** Two teenagers discussing a magazine article **Speaking:** Talking about experiences **Writing:** A text about exciting experiences
Buying presents / souvenirs **Pronunciation:** /h/	**Reading:** A short story **Listening:** A teenager talking about his reading habits **Speaking:** Talking about a book you have read recently **Writing:** A book review
Curriculum extra C, Literature: pages C5–C6	
Reporting a crime **Pronunciation:** /ə/	**Reading:** An extract from Sherlock Holmes: The Hound of the Baskervilles **Listening:** A police interview with a suspect **Speaking:** Talking about your favorite detective stories **Writing:** A text about your favorite detective
Discussing what things are for **Pronunciation:** /ð/	**Reading:** A biography of John Logie Baird **Listening:** Teenagers talking about old and new objects **Speaking:** Talking about your favorite objects **Writing:** A factfile about a famous inventor
Curriculum extra D, Math: pages C7–C8	

Welcome

Vocabulary
Physical descriptions

1 **Complete the descriptions with the words in the box.**

beard blond blue freckles glasses green heavy ~~tall~~ long mustache short ~~slim~~ spiky wavy

a She's tall and slim. She has [1]_________, [2]_________, red hair, and [3]_________ eyes. She wears [4]_________ and she has [5]_________ on her nose.

b He's [6]_________ and a little [7]_________. He has short, [8]_________, [9]_________ hair, and [10]_________ eyes. He has a [11]_________ and a [12]_________.

2 **And you?** **Write a short description of yourself and one person in your family.**

I'm tall and …
My grandma is short and …

Music

3 **Complete the names of the instruments.**

1 h a r p
2 p _ _ n _
3 r _ c _ r d _ r
4 s _ x _ p h _ n _
5 g _ _ t _ r
6 t r _ m p _ t
7 d r _ m s
8 v _ _ l _ n

4 **Listen and put the types of music in the correct order.**

1 classical ___
2 jazz ___
3 hip-hop ___
4 reggae a
5 rock ___
6 pop ___

5 **And you?** **What is your favorite kind of music? Who is your favorite singer / band?**

Jobs

6 **Complete the jobs with the words in the box.**

count dress elect fact in law off ~~or~~ our post

doctor
1 _______ory worker
2 hair_______er
3 j_______nalist
4 ac_______ant
5 _______rician
6 _______yer
7 _______ice worker
8 eng_______eer
9 _______al worker

7 **And you?** **What is your ideal job? Why?**

Movies

8 **Match the movies with the definitions.**

action movie ~~animated movie~~ comedy fantasy movie horror movie love story science fiction movie thriller

1 A movie with cartoon characters
animated movie
2 A very frightening movie with monsters
____
3 A movie about the future
____
4 A funny movie
____
5 A movie about an imaginary world
____
6 A movie about relationships and romance
____
7 A frightening movie with a lot of suspense
____
8 A movie with a lot of fast and exciting events
____

9 **And you?** **What is your favorite movie?**

Transportation

10 **Complete the chart with the words in the box.**

~~airplane~~ bike boat bus car
ferry helicopter motorcycle
subway taxi train truck

Air	Road

airplane	2 ______
1 ______	3 ______
	4 ______
	5 ______
	6 ______
	7 ______
Rail	**Water**

8 ______	10 ______
9 ______	11 ______

11 **And you?** **What forms of transportation do you use?**

Food and drink

12 **Complete Carla's shopping list. Match A and B to make food words.**

A	B
1 che	goes
2 cook	atoes
3 mi	na
4 bre	lk
5 man	ies
6 pot	er
7 sal	ese
8 tu	urt
9 wat	ad
10 yog	mon

13 **And you?** **What is your favorite food? What food don't you like?**

Geography

14 **Match words 1–6 with the geographical features a–f.**

1 desert d
2 lake ___
3 mountain ___
4 island ___
5 volcano ___
6 river ___

15 **And you?** **Can you name an example for each geographical feature?**

Feelings and emotions

16 **Look at the faces. Choose the correct words.**

1 excited / fed up

2 angry / bored

3 happy / sad

4 embarrassed / annoyed

5 confident / frightened

6 nervous / proud

17 **And you?** **How do you feel today?**

Grammar

Simple present / Present progressive

1 Complete the sentences with the simple present or present progressive form of the verbs in parentheses.

1 Manuel usually travels (travel) to school by bus, but this morning he [1]_________ (not go) by bus. His mom [2]_________ (take) him to school by car.

2 Mari and Kana [1]_________ (go) to the movies every Saturday. They usually [2]_________ (watch) love stories, but today they [3]_________ (watch) a thriller.

3 I [1]_________ (not like) vegetables, but my grandma always [2]_________ (cook) them for me. It's lunch time now and I [3]_________ (give) my vegetables to the dog!

4 A [1]_________ (Laura / play) any sports on the weekend?
B Yes, she does. She sometimes [2]_________ (play) basketball.
A [3]_________ (she / play) today?
B No, she isn't. She isn't on the team today so she [4]_________ (watch) the game.

2 Answer the questions with true answers.

1 How do you usually travel to school?
2 How often do you go to the movies?
3 Do you like vegetables?
4 What sports do you play every week?
5 Are you playing sports now?
6 What are you doing now?

be: Simple past

3 Robbie Smith is a music journalist. Write questions about his day yesterday. Then look at his schedule and answer the questions.

8 a.m.	Breakfast interview with Jay-Z at Café Gitane, New York.
10:30 a.m.	La Guardia Airport – New York.
11:30 a.m.	Airplane to Philadelphia
1:30 p.m.	Lunch with Jack Wilson of *Music Magazine* (Morimoto restaurant)
4 p.m.	Visit *The Rock* radio station with Jack
6 p.m.	Penn's View Hotel
8:30 p.m.	Lady Gaga concert – Susquehanna Bank Center, Camden

Robbie / be / in Camden / at 8 a.m. yesterday?
Was Robbie in Camden at 8 a.m. yesterday?
No, he wasn't. He was in New York.

1 Who / be / Robbie with / at 8 a.m?
____
____

2 Where / be / they?
____
____

3 What time / be / Robbie at the airport?
____
____

4 Where / be / Robbie and Jack Wilson / at 1:30 p.m?
____
____

5 They / be / in the restaurant / at 4:15 p.m?
____
____

6 Where / be / the Lady Gaga concert in the evening?
____
____

Simple past

4 Complete the text with the affirmative or negative simple past form of the verbs.

Sandra Carroll
Police officer

Yesterday morning I [1]__________ (go) to a school and [2]__________ (talk) about road safety. Then I [3]__________ (meet) a friend. We [4]__________ (not eat) lunch in a café. We [5]__________ (buy) some sandwiches and we [6]__________ (eat) them in the car. In the afternoon, I [7]__________ (write) some e-mails and I [8]__________ (make) some phone calls. I [9]__________ (finish) work at 5:30. I [10]__________ (not go out) in the evening. I [11]__________ (have) a relaxing evening at home.

5 Write questions about Sandra. Then answer the questions.

Where / Sandra / go yesterday morning?
Where did Sandra go yesterday morning?
She went to a school.

1 What / she / talk about?
____
____

2 Who / Sandra / meet after the talk?
____
____

3 What / they / buy for lunch?
____
____

4 Where / they / eat lunch?
____
____

5 What / she / do in the afternoon?
____
____

6 What time / she / finish work?
____
____

6 Complete the text with the simple past form of the verbs in the box.

become come go join make not have not speak start

Charlie Chaplin
One hundred years ago, movies were very different. Movie studios *made* them very quickly – sometimes in two or three days! They [1]__________ color – the images were black and white – and the actors [2]__________. This period of movie history is "The Silent Era". Charlie Chaplin was one of the great actors of the Silent Era. He [3]__________ from London and he [4]__________ his acting career in England. In 1910 he [5]__________ to the U.S. with a group of British actors. He [6]__________ the Keystone Film Company in 1914 and he soon [7]__________ a famous actor, writer, and movie director.

7 Read the answers. Complete the questions.

What period of movie history *did Charlie Chaplin act in*?
Charlie Chaplin acted in the period of movie history called "The Silent Era".

1 Where ______________?
He came from London in England.

2 When ______________?
He went to the U.S. in 1910.

3 What ______________ in 1914?
In 1914 he joined the Keystone Film Company.

4 What ______________?
He became a famous actor, writer, and movie director.

Present progressive for future

8 **Write questions with the present progressive. Then answer the questions.**

The Domes
Latin America Tour

February 26th	Buenos Aires, Argentina @ River Plate Stadium
February 28th	Rio de Janeiro, Brazil @ Apoteose Stadium
March 2nd	São Paulo, Brazil @ Morumbi Stadium
March 4th	Bogotá, Colombia @ Parque Simon Bolivar
March 6th	Mexico City, Mexico @ Foro Sol

Where / the tour / start?
Where is the tour starting?
It's starting in Buenos Aires.

1 When / the Domes / play / in Colombia?
____
2 How many / concerts / they / give / in Brazil?
____
3 Where / they / perform / in São Paulo?
____
4 Where / they / go / after Brazil?
____
5 Where / the tour / finish?
____
6 How many cities / they / visit / in Latin America?
____

How long ...? + take

9 **Write questions. Then answer the questions.**

How long / fly from Rio de Janeiro to São Paulo? (1 hour)
How long does it take to fly from Rio de Janeiro to São Paulo?
It takes one hour.

1 How long / drive from Rio de Janeiro to São Paulo? (7 hours)
2 How long / travel by airplane from Bogotá to Mexico City? (4 hours 45 minutes)
3 How long / go from São Paulo to Buenos Aires by bus? (2 days)

some / any with countable / uncountable nouns

10 **What food and drink is there in the refrigerator? Check (✓) or cross (✗) the food items, then write sentences.**

[✗] chicken *There isn't any chicken.*
[✓] carrots *There are some carrots.*
1 [ ] yogurt ______________
2 [ ] eggs ______________
3 [ ] cheese ______________
4 [ ] orange juice ______________
5 [ ] potatoes ______________

11 **Now write questions and short answers about the food in the refrigerator.**

water?
Is there any water? Yes, there is.

1 cookies? ______________
2 mangoes? ______________
3 salmon? ______________
4 tomatoes? ______________
5 beef? ______________

a lot of / much / many / a little / a few

12 **Choose the correct answers.**

Hi Ava!
I don't have (a lot of) / much free time because I always have [1]**a lot of / much** homework. I study twelve subjects at school. How [2]**much / many** subjects do you study? I don't watch [3]**much / many** TV because there aren't [4]**much / many** good shows on TV at the moment. I watch [5]**a little / a few** music shows. How [6]**much / many** TV shows do you watch? I listen to [7]**a lot of / much** music and I have [8]**many / a lot of** posters of my favorite bands on my bedroom wall. Do you have [9]**a lot of / many** posters? On the weekend, I often go for a pizza with my family. My favorite pizza is Four Cheeses. It has [10]**much / a lot of** cheese on it!

Comparative adjectives

13 **Complete the sentences with the comparative form of the adjectives.**

Luiza is older (old) than Beatriz.

1. Chicago is _________ (big) than Boston.
2. Traveling by bus is _________ (good) than traveling by train in South America.
3. Elephants are _________ (heavy) than giraffes.
4. San Francisco is _________ (far) from Mexico than San Diego.
5. Oxford is a _________ (safe) city than Detroit.
6. Is Colombia _________ (large) than Bolivia?
7. A documentary is _________ (interesting) than a quiz show.
8. Hawaii is _________ (hot) than Alaska.

Superlative adjectives

14 **Complete the sentences with the superlative form of the adjectives. Then write true answers.**

Who is the oldest (old) person in your family?
My grandma. She's 75 years old.

1. What is _________ (difficult) subject for you at school?
____
2. What is _________ (easy) subject for you at school?
____
3. Who is _________ (good) singer in your country?
____
4. What was _________ (bad) movie you saw last year?
____
5. What is _________ (famous) tourist attraction in your country?
____
6. Who is _________ (tall) person in your family?
____

15 **Complete the geography quiz with the comparative or the superlative form of the adjectives. Are the statements true (✓) or false (✗)?**

Geo quiz!

	T	F
1 Mount Everest is _________ (tall) mountain in the world.	☐	☐
2 The Pacific Ocean is _________ (deep) than the Atlantic Ocean.	☐	☐
3 South America is _________ (big) than North America.	☐	☐
4 The Mediterranean Sea is _________ (large) the Gulf of Mexico.	☐	☐
5 The Vatican City is _________ (small) country in the world.	☐	☐
6 China is _________ (populated) than the U.S.A.	☐	☐
7 The River Nile is _________ (long) river in Africa.	☐	☐
8 The Atacama Desert in Chile is _________ (dry) place in the world.	☐	☐

1 Nobody lives here

1 **Read and listen** **Check (✓) the correct description of the text.**

a an educational leaflet ☐ b a tourist leaflet ☐ c an online store ☐

2 **Comprehension** **Answer the questions.**

1 When was Calico a busy town?
2 What is unusual about it today?
3 What can you see in Main Street?
4 How can you travel around Calico?
5 Where can you stay in Calico?
6 Why can't you visit the old mines?

CALICO – A CALIFORNIAN GHOST TOWN

What was life like during the American silver and gold rush? How did people live? Come to the historic town of Calico and find out!

In the late 19th century people from all over the world traveled to California to look for silver and gold. They built small mining towns everywhere in the area. Calico was once a busy silver mining town with 500 silver mines. It had a population of 1,200 people and there were stores, hotels, cafés, a church, and a school. When the silver rush ended at the start of the 20th century, everybody left Calico and today nobody lives there!

Attractions

Calico is now a major tourist attraction. Walk down Main Street and look at the old stores and cafés. Turn right after Lil's saloon and visit Maggie's Mine, or take a ride around town on a mining train. And why not stay a few days? Calico has a luxury campground.

Calico has something for everyone! Come and discover it!

Visitors' guidelines

Please follow the town rules

1 The old mines in the area are very dangerous. You mustn't go near them.
2 You must keep your animals under control.
3 You mustn't drive in the town. Leave your car in the official parking lot.
4 You mustn't enter the private buildings or take anything from the town.
5 You must use the official picnic areas and you mustn't start fires.
6 You mustn't leave trash in the area. Take it home with you.

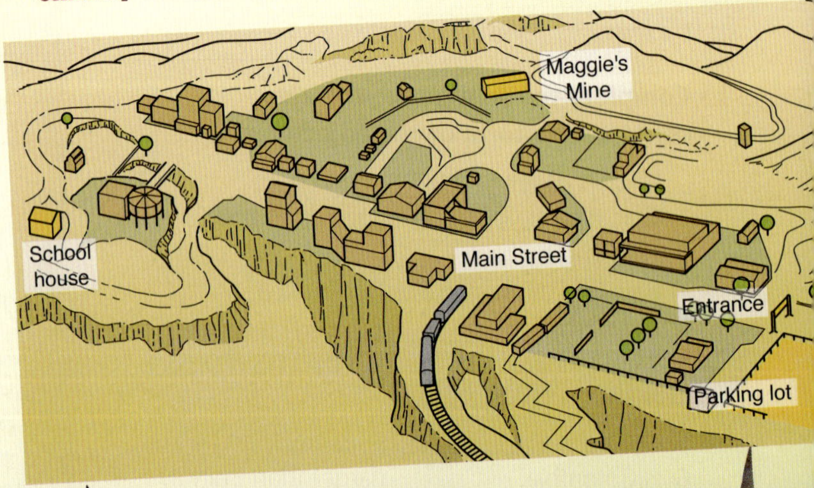

Language focus

3 **Look at the signs. Then read the text and write the rules.**

1 *You mustn't leave trash.*

2 ________________

3 ________________

4 ________________

5 ________________

6 ________________

4 **Look at the text again. Complete the sentences with the missing words.**

1 In the late 19th century people built small mining towns *everywhere* in the area
2 At the start of the 20th century __________ left Calico.
3 Today __________ lives there.
4 You mustn't take __________ from the town.
5 The town has __________ for __________!

5 **Focus on you** **Write what you must and mustn't do every day. Use the verbs in the box.**

be late for school   do my homework   go to school   stay out late
throw trash in the street   watch TV all day

I must go to school every day.
I mustn't stay out late.

6 **Pairwork** **Tell your partner what you must and mustn't do every day.**

Vocabulary

Places around town

1 **Match the words with the places on the map. Then listen and repeat.**

bank bus station bus stop ~~café~~ church hospital library park
parking lot police station post office shopping mall sports center

Look!

You borrow books from a **library**.
You buy books from a **bookstore**.

1 *café* 2 ________ 3 ________ 4 ________
5 ________ 6 ________ 7 ________ 8 ________
9 ________ 10 ________ 11 ________ 12 ________
13 ________

2 **Read the sentences and identify the places in the picture in exercise 1.**

It's between the library and the post office. *the bank*

1 It's in front of the shopping mall. ________
2 It's behind the bank. ________
3 It's next to the café. ________
4 It's on the corner of Main Street near the bank. ________
5 It's opposite the sports center. ________

3 **Pairwork** **Look at the map in exercise 1 and write three dialogues.**

bank / post office

A Excuse me. Where's the bank, please?
B It's on Main Street. It's near the post office.

1 park / shopping mall
2 hospital / sports center
3 library / bank
4 market / café
5 church / police station
6 park / bank

CD-ROM Workbook p.W4

must

Affirmative	
I / you / he / she / it / we / you / they	must stop
Negative	
I / you / he / she / it / we / you / they	mustn't (must not) stop

Think!

Read the sentences. Then choose the correct alternative.

You must come home now.
You mustn't play computer games.

- We use *must* / *mustn't* for [1]rules / requests.
- *must* / *mustn't* are the [2]same / different for all persons.
- *must* / *mustn't* are followed by the infinitive [3]with / without *to*.

Rules p.W2

1 Complete the rules for a school test. Use *must* and *mustn't*.

Test rules

You mustn't talk. (✗)
You ________ write your name on the test. (✓)
You ________ use a dictionary. (✗)
You ________ use a blue or black pen. (✓)
You ________ leave the room. (✗)
You ________ use your cell phones. (✗)

2 What do these signs mean? Complete the rules with *You must* / *You mustn't*.

1 You mustn't turn left.
2 ________________ stop.
3 ________________ park your car here.
4 ________________ turn right.
5 ________________ smoke here.
6 ________________ drive more than 50 km/h.

3 Complete the swimming pool rules. Use *must* or *mustn't* and the verbs in the box.

~~buy~~ eat listen take use walk

SPICEBALL SPORTS CENTER

SWIMMING POOL RULES

You must buy a ticket at reception.
1 You ________ a shower before you enter the swimming pool.
2 You ________ or drink in the swimming pool.
3 You ________ slowly near the swimming pool. Don't run!
4 You ________ cell phones in the swimming pool.
5 You ________ to loud music.

4 Rewrite the orders.

Don't park your car here!
You mustn't park your car here.
Stop at a red traffic light.
You must stop at a red traffic light.

1 Don't skateboard in the park!
____
2 Buy a ticket before you get on the train.
____
3 Don't talk loudly in the library.
____
4 Change your shoes before you go into the gym.
____
5 Leave your parking ticket in the car window.
____

Finished?

What must and mustn't you do at your school? Write five sentences.

You mustn't eat in class.
You must listen to the teacher.

CD-ROM Workbook p.W4

Communication

Asking for and giving directions

1 **Complete the dialogue with the words in the box. Listen and check. Then listen and repeat.**

bank ~~excuse me~~ park roundabout traffic lights

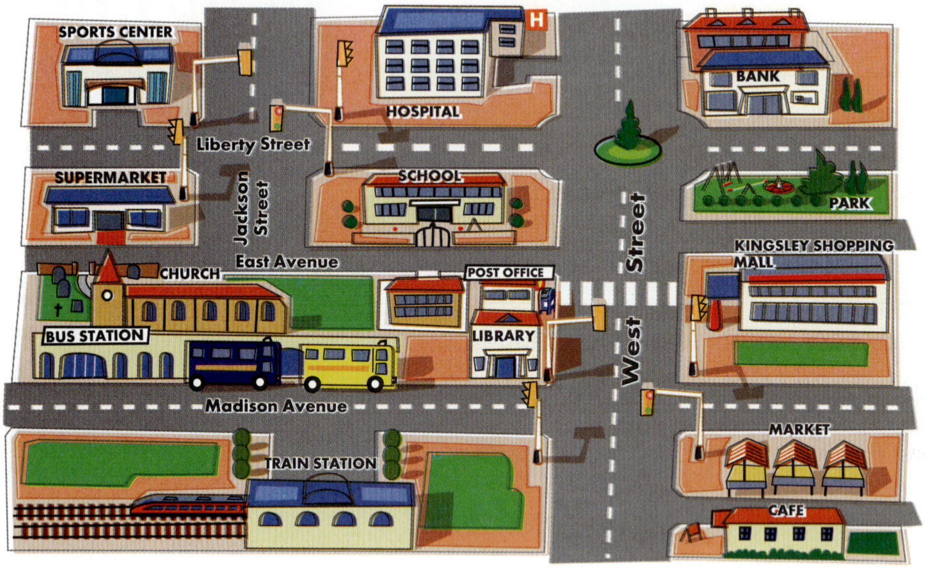

At the bus station

A Excuse me. How do I get to the bank, please?

B Go down Madison Avenue as far as the [1]_________. Turn left and go up West Street. Go straight on at the [2]_________ and the [3]_________ is on the right. It's opposite the [4]_________.

A Thanks.

You ask	You answer
Excuse me. How do I get to …, please?	Go straight on at … / Cross over the road … Turn right / left. Go down the road to … Take the first / second turning on the right / left. It's on the right / left.
Excuse me. Can you tell me the way to …, please?	Go up / down this road as far as / to … Go to the end of this / the road.

2 Pronunciation **Listen to the pronunciation of the letter *r*. Then listen and repeat.**

church far library market over park right road street turn

3 **Listen to three people giving directions to the places below. Follow the directions on the map in exercise 1 and write the names of the places.**

1 From the sports center to the ____________________.
2 From the hospital to the ____________________.
3 From the shopping mall to the ____________________.

4 Pairwork **Look at the map in exercise 1 and write two dialogues. Then practice your dialogues.**

1 You are at the market. Ask for directions to the church.
2 You are at the school. Ask for directions to the train station.

CD-ROM Workbook p.W6

Grammar

Compounds: *some / any / no*

	Person	Thing	Place
some	someone / somebody	something	somewhere
any	anyone / anybody	anything	anywhere
no	no one / nobody	nothing	nowhere

Think!

Read the sentences. Then complete the rules with *affirmative*, *negative*, and *interrogative*.

There's someone coming.
I can't do anything!
Did you go anywhere on the weekend?
I have nothing to do.

- We use compounds of *some* in [1]________ sentences.
- We use compounds of *any* in [2]________ and [3]________ sentences.
- We use compounds of *no* with the [4]________ form of a verb.

Rules pp.W2–W3

1 Choose the correct answers.

I'm not doing **nothing / anything** today.
1 I don't know **anyone / no one** here.
2 There's **something / anything** I want to ask you.
3 Are you going **somewhere / anywhere** exciting on the weekend?
4 **No one / Anyone** ever listens to me!
5 Where's Ruby? She isn't **anywhere / nowhere** in the library.
6 There isn't **someone / anyone** in the bank.

2 Complete the sentences with *some*, *any*, and *no* compounds.

Look! There's someone at the door.
1 Let's go ________ nice on Sunday.
2 There's ________ in the refrigerator to eat! Let's order a pizza.
3 I didn't see ________ from school at the concert.
4 I'm bored! I don't have ________ to do.
5 This town is boring. There's ________ to go.
6 Where's the dog? I can't see him ________.

Compounds: *every*

	Person	Thing	Place
every	everyone / everybody	everything	everywhere

Think!

Read the sentences. Then choose the correct alternatives.

Everybody makes mistakes.
We didn't go everywhere in Paris.
Do you have everything for your vacation?

1 We can use compounds of *every* in:
a affirmative ☐ / b negative ☐ / c interrogative ☐ sentences.
2 We use *everyone / everybody* with a
a singular ☐ / b plural ☐ verb.

Rules p.W3

3 Complete the sentences with *everyone / everybody*, *everything*, and *everywhere*.

Everyone in my class is fourteen years old.
1 I had a fantastic time! I went ________!
2 Maria's very popular. ________ likes her.
3 Did you eat ________ at lunch today?
4 A Is ________ here today?
B No, Karen is absent.
5 A Here are the ingredients for the apple pie.
B Do we have ________?
6 ________ in my family likes fish.

4 Game! Find people who did the things below. Write their names in the chart.

Find someone who ...	Name
went somewhere last weekend	
sent a text message yesterday	
met someone after school yesterday	

A Did you go anywhere last weekend, Alan?
B No, I didn't.
A Did you go anywhere last weekend, Isabel?
C Yes, I did. I went to the mountains.

Finished?

Look at the list in exercise 4 again. What things did you do and what things didn't you do?

I didn't go anywhere last weekend, but I sent someone a text message yesterday ...

CD-ROM Workbook p.W5

Stay safe online!

Everyone loves the Internet! You can do a lot of great things online: play games, download music, or read about your favorite band. However, the Internet isn't always safe. Nobody controls the information on it and everyone can use it. Here are a few rules to keep you safe online.

- You must keep your passwords secret. Don't share them with your friends and don't store them in a file on your computer. People can use your passwords to enter websites that you use and find information about you.
- You mustn't open a file, message, or photo from someone you don't know. Sometimes these things contain viruses and they can damage your computer.
- Only give personal information on safe sites. You mustn't give anyone your name, address, or phone number if you don't know them.
- You mustn't put your photos on public sites. Anyone can look at them and sometimes people copy photos from the Internet and use them for the wrong things.
- If someone on the Internet asks you to meet them, you must say no and tell your parents. Some people don't tell the truth on the Internet and invent information. It can be very dangerous to meet online "friends". You must tell your parents or an adult if you aren't sure about anything.

Reading

1 Before you read **Discuss the questions with the class.**

1 What do you use the Internet for?
2 What Internet sites do you look at?

2 Read the text. Then answer the questions.

1 What different things can you do online?
2 Why isn't the Internet always safe?
3 Why must you keep your passwords secret?
4 What do files or photos sometimes contain?
5 When is it safe to give personal information online?
6 When isn't it safe to give personal information online?
7 Why is it a bad idea to put your photos on public sites?
8 Why is it a bad idea to meet online "friends"?

Listening

3 **Listen to Denzel Wilcox, a police officer, speak about how to be safe on the roads today. Then complete the Dos and Don'ts for cyclists. Use the words in the box.**

clothes correct side of the road friends hand signals ~~helmet~~ music road signs shoes

Do	Don't
You must wear a helmet.	

Speaking

4 **Pairwork** **Look at the following categories of road users. Discuss the rules of the road for each category. Make a list of two rules, one with *must* and one with *mustn't*, for each person. Then present your list to the class.**

A Pedestrians must look left and right before crossing the road.
B Pedestrians mustn't cross the road when a traffic light is red.

Writing

5 **Choose one of the categories in exercise 4 and write a short paragraph describing road safety rules. Remember to talk about general road rules and include the points below:**

- clothes
- cell phones
- music
- eating and drinking

CD-ROM Workbook p.W7

2 I have to clean my room

1 Read and listen Match the paragraphs with the contents.

1 Paragraph 1	a The hosts
2 Paragraph 2	b Housework advice
3 Paragraph 3	c This week's episode
4 Paragraph 4	d The TV series

1 **Kim Woodburn and Aggie Mackenzie are on a mission.** They want to clean the world! Kim and Aggie are the stars of the TV series *How Clean Is Your House?* In the show the two ladies go to dirty homes, clean them, and teach people how to do housework. The show is already a hit in the U.K, Germany, France, Spain, and the U.S. Kim says the show is a success because cleaning is an important part of everyone's life.

2 Before Kim and Aggie were TV hosts, Kim was a professional cleaner and Aggie worked for a magazine. Doing housework is their passion. Aggie likes cooking and she loves cleaning the kitchen, but she hates making beds. Kim likes doing the dusting, but she hates cleaning the bathtub. "It's like cleaning seven sinks!" she says.

3 In this week's episode of *How Clean Is Your House?* Kim and Aggie visit the house of four students. They hate doing housework. They never wash the dishes, clean the bathroom, make the beds, or take out the trash. Their house is a mess! Teaching them the basics of housework isn't easy, but Kim and Aggie succeed and in twenty-four hours the students have a clean house.

4 So what are the secrets to a clean house?

REPETITION! You have to clean every day. You don't have to spend a lot of time cleaning – thirty minutes a day is enough.

ORGANIZATION! Everything has to have a place.

ELIMINATION! You have to throw out things you don't need or use.

2 Comprehension Answer the questions.

1 What is Kim and Aggie's mission?
2 What do Kim and Aggie do in their TV series?
3 What did Kim and Aggie do before they were TV hosts?
4 Where do Kim and Aggie go in this week's episode?
5 Why is the house a mess?
6 What are the three key words in housework?

Language focus

3 Hana is one of the students in this week's episode of *How Clean Is Your House?* Listen and complete the sentences with *have to* or *don't have to*.

You have to do some housework every day.
1 You ________ make the beds, clean the kitchen and bathroom, and do the dusting.
2 You ________ throw out things you don't need.
3 When you do housework everyday you ________ spend a lot of time cleaning.
4 You ________ spend a lot of money on cleaning products.
5 Kim and Aggie say you ________ take care of your house and enjoy it!

4 Look at the photos and read the text again. What chores do Kim and Aggie like doing and hate doing?

1 Aggie loves cleaning the kitchen.

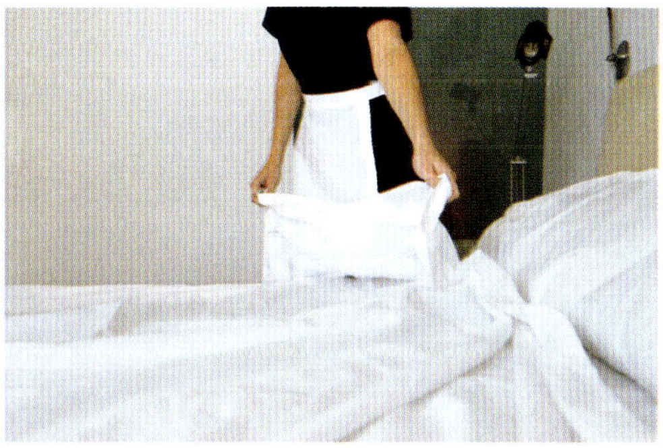

2 ____________________

3 ____________________

4 ____________________

5 Focus on you Write a dialogue about what you like doing and hate doing. Use the words in the box.

clean the bathtub clean the kitchen cook do housework
do the dusting go to the library make your bed take out the trash

A I hate doing housework.
B So do I.
A I like cooking.
B Really? I don't!

6 Pairwork Practice the dialogues from exercise 5.

2

Vocabulary

Housework

1 **Listen and match the words in the box with the pictures. Then listen and repeat.**

clean my room | clean the bathroom | do the cooking | do the dusting | do the grocery shopping | do the ironing | do the washing | lay / clear the table | load / unload the dishwasher | ~~make my bed~~ | take out the trash | wash the dishes

1 – make my bed

2 **Complete the sentences with the verbs from exercise 1.**

I always *clear* the table after lunch.

1 I _________ my bed when I get up in the morning.
2 We _________ the grocery shopping at the supermarket.
3 I usually _________ my bedroom on the weekend.
4 My dad _________ out the trash every evening.
5 I _____ the dishwasher after dinner and my sister _________ it.
6 My dad sometimes _________ the cooking on the weekend.
7 My sister _________ the dishes after lunch.
8 My mom listens to music when she _________ the ironing.

3 **Pairwork** **Ask your partner how often he / she does the housework in exercise 1. Use the expressions in the box.**

every day | never | often | once / twice a week | rarely

A How often do you clean your room?
B I clean my room once a week. How often do you do the ironing?
A I rarely do the ironing.

Grammar

have to
Affirmative and negative

	Affirmative	Negative
I / you / we / you / they	have to go	don't have to go
he / she / it	has to go	doesn't have to go

Think!

- **Read the sentences. Then choose the correct alternative.**

  I have to stay in my room.

  You don't have to clean your room.

- *have to* and *don't have to* are followed by the *-ing* form / infinitive without *to* of the main verb.

Rules p.W8

1 Jenny and Simon go to different schools. Write sentences about what they have to or don't have to do.

Jenny has to wear (wear) a uniform. (✓)
Simon doesn't have to wear (wear) a uniform. (✗)

1 Jenny ________ (do) a test every week. (✗)
2 Jenny and Simon ________ (have) lunch at school. (✓)
3 Simon ________ (do) two hours of homework every day. (✓)
4 Simon ________ (play) sports on Saturday. (✓)
5 Jenny ________ (be) at school at 7:00 a.m. (✗)
6 Jenny and Simon ________ (stand up) when a teacher comes into the classroom. (✗)

2 Do you have to or don't you have to do these things at your school? Write sentences.

wear a uniform?
I have to wear a uniform. / I don't have to wear a uniform.

1 Have lunch at school?
2 Do a test every week?
3 Play sports on Saturday?
4 Do two hours of homework every day?
5 Switch off cell phones during lessons?
6 Stand up when a teacher enters the classroom?

have to
Interrogative and short answers

Interrogative	Short answers	
	Affirmative	Negative
Do I / you **have to go**?	Yes, I / you **do**.	No, I / you **don't**.
Do we / you / they **have to go**?	Yes, we / you / they **do**.	No, we / you / they **don't**.
Does he / she / it **have to go**?	Yes, he / she / it **does**.	No, he / she / it **doesn't**.

Rules p.W8

3 Write questions about what Ryan and Jess have to and don't have to do. Then answer the questions.

Jess / do the dusting? (✓)
Does Jess have to do the dusting? Yes, she does.

1 Ryan / do the ironing (✓)
2 Jess and Ryan / wash the dishes (✓)
3 Jess and Ryan / lay the table (✗)
4 Jess / do the washing (✗)
5 Ryan / take out the trash (✓)

4 Complete the questions with *have to* and the verbs in the box. Then answer the questions.

be be clean do get up ~~go~~

What time do you have to go to bed on school nights?
I have to go to bed at 9:30 p.m.

1 How many hours of homework ________ every day?
2 What time ________ home in the evenings on school days?
3 How often ________ your bedroom?
4 What time ________ in the morning on school days?
5 How old ________ to drive a car in your country?

Finished?

Write a list of the housework you have to or don't have to do.

I don't have to do the cooking.

CD-ROM Workbook p.W10

Asking for permission

1 Listen and complete the sentences. Then listen and repeat.

1

Jennifer	Mom, can I go to Susan's house?
Mom	I'm sorry, you can't, Jennifer. You have to clean your room.
Jennifer	But Mom we have to do our science project.
Mom	Jennifer, your room is a mess!
Jennifer	But doing my science project is more important.
Mom	Clean your room first. Then you can go to Susan's house.
Jennifer	Mom! I hate cleaning my room!
Mom	Jennifer!

Jennifer wants to ________.

2

Kenny	Miss Harper.
Miss Harper	Yes, what is it, Kenny?
Kenny	May I go to the bathroom, please?
Miss Harper	Not now, Kenny. You have to wait.

Kenny wants to ________.

Look!
May I ...? is more formal than *Can I ...?*

You ask	You answer
Can I go to Susan's house, (please)?	Yes, you can. / No, you can't. / No, I'm sorry, you can't.
May I go to the bathroom, (please)?	Yes, of course. / Sure. / OK.

2 Pronunciation Listen to the pronunciation of *have* /hæv/ and *have to* /ˈhæf tə/. Then listen and repeat.

In the expression ***have to*** the /v/ sound in *have* becomes an /f/ sound.
/hæv/ I **have** lunch at school.
/ˈhæf tə/ I **have to** finish my homework.

3 Listen and write (*a*) /hæv/ or (*b*) /ˈhæf tə/. Then listen and repeat.

1 a 2 __ 3 __
4 __ 5 __ 6 __

4 Pairwork Write a dialogue for these situations. Then practice your dialogues.

1 You ask your friend if you can use his / her cell phone. You say that you have to send a text message and you don't have any credit. Your friend agrees.
2 You ask your mom if you can go to your friend's house. You explain that you have to study for a history test tomorrow. Your mom says no. You have to wash the dishes and finish your homework.

CD-ROM Workbook p.W12

Grammar

mustn't / don't have to

Think!

Read the sentences. Choose the correct alternative.

- It's Sunday tomorrow. We [1]*mustn't / don't have to* go to school.
- The traffic lights are green. You [2]*mustn't / don't have to* cross the road.

Rules p.W9

1 Complete the sentences with *mustn't* or *don't / doesn't have to*.

You <u>*don't have to*</u> pass a test to ride a bike.
You <u>*mustn't*</u> use your cell phone in class.

1 You ________ copy during the test!
2 It's Sunday! I ________ get up early.
3 The movie starts at 8 p.m. Hurry up! We ________ be late!
4 You ________ speak to the driver on the bus. It's dangerous.
5 It's free! You ________ buy a ticket!
6 He's a millionaire. He ________ work.
7 Cooking pasta is easy. You ________ be a chef!

Gerunds

Think!

Circle the gerunds in the sentences.

1 Drinking a lot of coffee is bad for you.
2 Doing housework is boring.
3 Learning a new language is interesting.

Rules p.W9

2 Complete the sentences with the gerund form of the verbs in the box.

do go learn ~~play~~ play read watch

<u>*Playing*</u> chess is difficult.
1 ________ homework is boring.
2 ________ languages is useful.
3 ________ a book is more interesting than ________ TV.
4 ________ to a foreign country is exciting.
5 ________ sports is good for you.

Verb + *-ing* form

	love	
	like	
	enjoy	
I	prefer	cooking.
	don't mind	
	don't like	
	hate	

Rules p.W9

3 Write sentences.

I / love / go to the movies.
I love going to the movies.
1 He / hate / play chess.
2 You / like / read comics?
3 We / not mind / go bowling / but / we / hate / skateboard.
4 My dad / enjoy / listen to classical music.
5 I / not like / watch documentaries.

4 Game! How well do you know your partner? Complete the table with faces.

☺ = LIKE ☹̶ = DON'T MIND ☹ = HATE

	YOUR PARTNER
Doing the cooking	
Washing the dishes	
Going shopping	
Swimming	
Playing sports	
Listening to music	
Going to the movies	
Getting up early	

Compare your answers and give yourself 1 point for each correct answer.

You like swimming.
No, I don't! I hate swimming!

Your score

6–8 Good job! You know your partner very well.
3–5 OK. You have to learn to listen more.
1–2 May I introduce you to … .

Write about your partner's likes and dislikes.

Ryo doesn't mind washing the dishes, but he hates going shopping …

CD-ROM Workbook pp.W10–W11

Lazy teenagers? Think again!

Are today's teenagers lazy? According to a recent survey, teenagers spend a total of fifty hours doing after-school activities, homework, and chores.

Teenager, Jessica Watson, isn't surprised. "I go to school from 8:30 a.m. to 3:30 p.m. But after school I don't go home and watch TV. I'm on the school volleyball team so I have to practice twice a week on Tuesdays and Fridays. I also go to ballet lessons on Thursdays."

At home Jessica helps with the housework. "Both my parents work and they often get home late. I have to clean my room, take out the trash, and do the dusting. Mom does the grocery shopping and the cooking, and Dad washes the dishes."

Jessica also spends a lot of time doing homework. "I have to do two or three hours of homework every night," says Jessica. This is normal for teenagers today. On average, they spend about nine hours a week doing homework.

On Saturdays and Sundays, Jessica has a part-time job in a clothes store. "Mom and Dad don't give me an allowance, so I have to work to get money for clothes, CDs, and going out with my friends. I like spending the money, but I hate getting up early for work on weekends."

Jessica hates it when adults say teenagers are lazy. "Adults think we watch TV, listen to music, and send text messages all the time. But this isn't true. I enjoy doing those things, but I do a lot of other things, too."

Reading

1 Before you read Discuss the questions with a partner.

1 What do you do in your free time?
2 Do you have to help at home?

2 Read the text. Then answer the questions.

1 How many hours a week do teenagers spend doing after-school activities, homework, and housework?
2 What after-school activities does Jessica do?
3 How often does she go to volleyball practice?
4 What housework does she do?
5 Who does the grocery shopping, cooking, and who washes the dishes in her family?
6 How many hours do teenagers spend doing homework in a week?
7 What does Jessica do on weekends?
8 What do adults generally think of teenagers? Is this true?

Listening

3 **Listen to the conversation about boys and housework. Are the sentences true or false? Correct the false sentences.**

Robert says that boys don't do housework. F
Robert says that boys do lots of housework.

1 Robert doesn't have to clean his room.
2 Robert doesn't do the cooking.
3 Robert usually clears the table.
4 Julie says that boys do lots of housework.
5 Julie cleans her brother's room.
6 Yesterday Julie's brother had to wash the dishes and take the dog for a walk.

Speaking

4 **Pairwork** **Ask and answer questions about housework. Ask your partner if he / she likes doing these jobs.**

Do you have to …?

- make your bed
- wash the car
- lay / clear the table
- take out the trash
- clean your room
- do the cooking
- take the dog for a walk
- do the ironing
- wash the dishes
- load / unload the dishwasher
- do the washing

A Do you have to make your bed?
B Yes, I do.
A Do you like making your bed?
B No, I don't. I hate making my bed.

5 **Now prepare a short report about your partner.**

- Carlos / Isabel has to …
- He / She likes …
- He / She enjoys …
- He / She doesn't mind …
- He / She hates …

Writing

6 **Complete the chart with information about your weekly schedule. Then write a short paragraph about what you do. Use the text on page 24 as a model.**

How many hours do you spend	Hours a week
• at school?	____
• doing homework?	____
• doing after-school activities (sports, clubs, music, etc.)?	____
• doing housework?	____

I'm not a lazy teenager! I have to …

CD-ROM Workbook p.W13

A Review

Vocabulary

1 Look at the things Lisa wants to do. Complete the names of the places she needs to visit.

Things to do	Places
1 get some money	b*an*k
2 borrow a book	l______y
3 play tennis	s______s c______r
4 visit Jane and her new baby	h______l
5 send a letter	p______t o______e
6 buy new clothes	s______g m______l
7 have lunch	c______é
8 sit in the sun	p______k
9 buy some bus tickets	b______s s______n
10 get the bus home	b______s s______p

2 What housework tasks do these objects relate to? Complete the verbs.

1 do the *cooking*

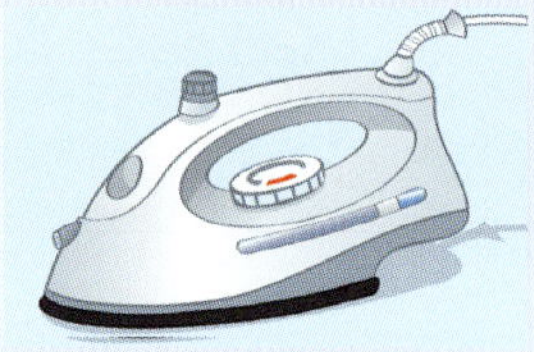

2 do the ________

3 ________ the trash

4 wash ________

5 ________ the table

6 ________ the grocery shopping

7 unload ________

8 do ________

Grammar

3 Complete the rules with *must / mustn't* and the verbs in the box.

cycle leave play take use ~~wait~~ walk

You *must wait* here.

1 You ________ photos.

2 You ________ soccer in the park.

3 You ________ the trash cans.

4 You ________ here.

5 You ________ trash on the bus.

4 Complete the sentences with the correct compound of *some / any / no / every*.

Mari said *something* interesting.

1 They didn't go ____________ on Saturday. They stayed at home.
2 Julia met ____________ nice yesterday.
3 ____________ went to Harry's party. It was great!
4 There's ____________ good on TV tonight. Let's watch a DVD.
5 Is ____________ ready? Let's go!
6 My cell phone is ____________ in the living room, but I can't find it.

5 **Read the advertisement. Then complete the e-mail with *have to / don't have to* and the verbs in the box.**

ask bring ~~be~~ have pay pay

SOCCER SUMMER SCHOOL!

Ridgewell Sports Center (July 11 – 15)

Beginners are welcome.

Price: $80 per person. Price includes lunch and drinks.
Bring your own sneakers, shorts, and T-shirts.
Participants must have a medical certificate.

Hi, Jason
Fantastic news! There's a Soccer Summer School at Ridgewell Sports Center in July! You _don't have to be_ good at soccer – beginners are welcome. You ¹_______________ $80, but you ²_______________ extra for lunch. You ³_______________ your own sneakers, shorts, and T-shirts and you ⁴_______________ a medical certificate. I really want to go, but I ⁵_______________ my dad for the money! Are you interested?
Ross

6 **Complete the sentences with *mustn't, don't have to,* or *doesn't have to.***

I _don't have to_ iron my clothes. Mom irons them.
You _mustn't_ leave dirty dishes in the sink!

1 Be careful! You _________ use a hot iron for this sweater. It's very delicate!
2 I have to lay the table, but I _________ clear it.
3 You _________ walk dogs in the park. It is a park for children only.
4 Mom _________ cook on Sunday. Dad cooks lunch.
5 You _________ run in the school corridors.
6 We _________ wash the dishes. We have a dishwasher!

7 **Write sentences.**

I / not mind / do / housework.
I don't mind doing housework.

1 Dad / hate / do / the shopping
2 we enjoy / work / in the yard
3 you / like / read?
4 learn / English / not be / difficult
5 I prefer / swim / to / play tennis
6 your mom / enjoy / cook?
7 Emi / not mind / study
8 watch / TV / be / fun

Got it?

8 **Read about Callum's job. Then choose the correct answers.**

I have a part-time job. I deliver newspapers to people's houses. I work Monday through Friday. Luckily, I **mustn't / (don't have to)** work on the weekend. I ¹**have to / have** get up at 6:30 a.m., but I don't mind ²**to get / getting up** early. I start work at 7 a.m. In California you ³**mustn't / don't have to** work before 7 a.m. or after 7 p.m. until you are sixteen years old. I have to ⁴**finish / finishing** work by 8 a.m. because I ⁵**mustn't / don't have to** be late for school. At 8 a.m. I go home, have ⁶**something / anything** to eat, and get ready for school. ⁷**Work / Working** in the mornings is sometimes difficult, but I love ⁸**do / doing** my paper round and I'm saving a lot of money!

9 **Answer the questions.**

1 What does Callum do before he goes to school?
2 How many days a week does he have to work?
3 What time does he have to get up?
4 Why does he have to finish his job by 8 a.m?
5 What does he do at 8 a.m?
6 Why does Sam love doing his paper round?

A Culture club

New York!

New York is a famous city on the east coast of the United States. Today it's very big and it has a population of eight million people, but in the 17th century it was very small. Only 270 people lived there! The city started on an island in the Hudson River. A group of Native Americans settled on the island and called it "Manhatta". This means "large island" in their language. Today the island's name is Manhattan. It is one of the five boroughs of New York. The other four boroughs are Staten Island, Brooklyn, Queens, and the Bronx. In 1624, the Dutch arrived in Manhatta and soon after, in 1664, the British took control of the area and called the city New York. In the 18th and 19th centuries a lot of people from Europe and Asia came to America to start a new life. A lot of immigrants settled in New York. People with the same nationality often lived in the same areas. For example, Chinese people created Chinatown and Italians created Little Italy.

Today there are also a lot of Hispanic people in the city. They come from Central and South America and they speak Spanish. Spanish is the first language in some areas of the city, but New York residents speak 170 different languages and 36% of the population was born in a different country! The mix of nationalities means that New York is a very exciting place. There is always something to do night and day. In fact, New York is also often called "the city that never sleeps!"

1 Before you read **Answer the question. Then read the text and check your answer.**

Which of these names is an old name for New York City?

a Manhatta b New Hudson c Little Italy

2 Answer the questions.

1 Where is New York?
2 What is the population of the city?
3 What is the name of its river?
4 What are the five boroughs of New York?
5 Where did people travel from in the 18th and 19th centuries?
6 Where do a lot of the immigrants come from today?
7 What language is the first language in some areas of New York?
8 How many languages do New York residents speak?

3 Focus on you **Write about a city that you know well. Answer the questions.**

- What is the name of the city and where is it?
- What do you know about its history?
- What are the names of the different areas of the city?
- Does it have a river? What is its name?
- What nationalities are the people and what is the first language?

My progress

A

Speaking and writing

1 I can identify different buildings on a map. **A2**

bank
1 ______
2 ______
3 ______
4 ______
5 ______

Got it? ___ / 5

2 I can ask for and give directions. **B1**

Excuse me. How do I get to the park?
1 ______
2 ______
3 ______
4 ______
5 ______

Got it? ___ / 5

3 I can talk about road safety rules. **B1**

You must wear a safety helmet.
1 ______
2 ______
3 ______
4 ______
5 ______

Got it? ___ / 5

4 I can identify different types of housework. **A2**

clean the bathroom
1 ______
2 ______
3 ______
4 ______
5 ______

Got it? ___ / 5

5 I can ask for and give permission. **B1**

Can I go to Tim's house?
1 ______
2 ______
3 ______
4 ______
5 ______

Got it? ___ / 5

6 I can ask people what housework they have to do. **B1**

Do you have to make your bed?
1 ______
2 ______
3 ______
4 ______
5 ______

Got it? ___ / 5

Reading, listening, and writing

			Got it?	
		Yes	I'm not sure	No
7 I can read and understand a text about a ghost town.	B1	☐	☐	☐
8 I can listen to a police officer talking about road safety.	B1	☐	☐	☐
9 I can read and understand a text about housework.	B1	☐	☐	☐
10 I can write about a city I know.	B1	☐	☐	☐

3 What are you going to do?

1 **Read and listen** **Match the names of the people with the jobs.**

1 Ashley a Computer games designer
2 Ly b Circus acrobat
3 Gilberto c Events organizer

Most young people want to be teachers, lawyers, or doctors, but some have more unusual ambitions. Read about three teenagers with big plans for the future.

I'd like to be an acrobat in a circus. It's the perfect job for me because I'm outgoing, confident, and hard-working. At the moment, I'm preparing for my career with the circus. I'm doing gymnastics lessons and ballet lessons and I'm going to start martial arts classes soon. This summer I'm going to take part in a circus summer camp, and when I finish school I hope to study at the Circus Center in San Francisco.
ASHLEY (15), U.S.

I want to be an events organizer and prepare events like weddings, parties, exhibitions, and festivals. I think I have the right qualities for the job. I'm ambitious, organized, and friendly. I'm going to get some important experiences for my job this summer. My best friend Cam is sixteen in July and I'm going to organize a birthday party for her. I hope to invite over 100 people! It's going to be a lot of work, but it's going to be fun!
LY (16), VIETNAM

I want to be a computer games designer. I'm very patient, but I'm creative, too. When I finish High School I'm going to study Games Programming. I'd like to go to the University of São Paulo because it has an excellent ICT department. I'm going to get a job this summer. I'd like to work as a games tester and test new computer games. I want to save some money for college.
GILBERTO (16) BRAZIL

2 Comprehension **Answer the questions.**

1 What is the perfect job for Ashley?
2 How is she preparing for her career now?
3 What does an events organizer do?
4 When is Cam having her birthday party?
5 Why does Gilberto want to go to the University of São Paulo?
6 What does a games tester do?

Language focus

3 Write sentences about Ashley, Ly, and Gilberto.

Ashley is going to start martial arts classes soon.

Ashley		organize a big birthday party.
		take part in a circus summer camp.
Ly	is going to	start martial arts classes soon.
		do a degree in Games Programming.
		get important job experience this summer.
Gilberto		get a summer job.

4 Read the article again. Then complete the sentences.

I'*d like to be* an acrobat in a circus.
1 I ________ at the Circus Center in San Francisco.

2 I ________ an events organizer!
3 I ________ over 100 people.

4 I ________ to the University of São Paulo.
5 I ________ some money for college.

5 Focus on you **Think about your plans for the future. Use the ideas in the box.**

get a summer job	learn more languages	learn to drive
make lots of money	study English at college	travel around the world

I'm going to / I'm not going to study English at college.
I'd like to learn to drive.

6 Pairwork **Tell your partner about your plans for the future.**

Vocabulary

Personality

1 Are the adjectives *Positive* (P) or *Negative* (N) or *Both* (B)? Use a dictionary.

1 ambitious P
2 bossy ___
3 confident ___
4 creative ___
5 friendly ___
6 hard-working ___
7 kind ___
8 lazy ___
9 organized ___
10 outgoing ___
11 patient ___
12 selfish ___
13 serious ___
14 shy ___
15 stubborn ___

2 Listen and repeat the adjectives in exercise 1.

3 Choose an adjective to describe these people.

Melissa "Peter never studies" He's lazy.
1 Laura "I'm nervous when I meet new people." _________
2 Daniel "I love parties and meeting new people.' _________
3 Larry "I never change my mind." _________
4 Rebecca "I draw and paint and write stories." _________
5 Steven "I think it's important to be good to people and to help them." _________
6 Sandra "I like giving orders and telling people what to do." _________

4 Pairwork Describe and identify the people in the photos.

A He's hard-working and serious.
B Number 1?
A Yes, that's right.

1

2

3

4

5

6

5 Pairwork Discuss your personality.

A What's the best thing about your personality?
B I'm outgoing.
A What's the worst thing?
B I'm lazy!

CD-ROM Workbook p.W16

be going to (1)
Affirmative and negative

Affirmative	Negative
I **am going to** leave	I**'m not going to** leave
you **are going to** leave	you **aren't going to** leave
he / she / it **is going to** leave	he / she / it **isn't going to** leave
we / you / they **are going to** leave	we / you / they **aren't going to** leave

Think!

Read the sentences. Then choose the correct alternative.

He**'s going to** watch TV tonight.
I**'m going to** write a book.

- We use *be going to* to talk about our intentions / present time activities.

Rules p.W14

1 Complete the sentences with *be going to* and the verbs in parentheses.

Pete's hungry. He *'s going to make* (make) a sandwich.

1 Tania's really outgoing. She _________ (invite) everybody in our class to her party!
2 I _________ (not play) tennis with Peter again! He always wins!
3 John and Peter want to learn karate. They _________ (take) lessons next month.
4 We're not hungry. We _________ (not have) a big lunch.
5 Jessica _________ (stay) with her aunt and uncle next summer.
6 I've seen this movie before. I _________ (not watch) it again.

be going to
Interrogative and short answers

Interrogative		
Am	I	**going to** leave?
Is	he / she / it	**going to** leave?
Are	you	**going to** leave?
Are	we / you / they	**going to** leave?

Short answers	
Affirmative	**Negative**
Yes, you **are**.	**No**, you **aren't**.
Yes, I **am**.	**No**, I**'m not**.
Yes, he / she / it **is**.	**No**, he / she / it **isn't**.
Yes, we / you / they **are**.	**No**, we / you / they **aren't**.

Rules p.W14

2 Read the answers. Then complete the questions.

Where *are they going to have dinner*?
They're going to have dinner at my aunt's.

1 How many days _______________?
We're going to stay in Mexico for a week.
2 When _______________?
They're going to play tennis on Saturday.
3 Where _______________?
They're going to go to Miami for Christmas.
4 How much _______________?
He's going to pay $1,200 for a new computer.
5 Which dress _______________?
She's going to buy the blue dress.
6 What _______________?
I'm going to have a sandwich for lunch.

3 Game! Which cities are the people going to visit?

Carlos is going to visit New York.

1 Carlos
2 Sue
3 Edson
4 Maki and Jun
5 Mark

Los Angeles
Paris
Rome
New York
Rio de Janeiro

Finished?

Write about your plans for the weekend. Write three things that you're going to do and three things you aren't going to do this weekend.

This weekend I'm going to …

CD-ROM Workbook pp. W16–W17

Communication

Inviting people to do things

1 **Complete the dialogues with the words in the box. Listen and check. Then listen and repeat.**

busy can't cool ~~free~~ have dinner look love sure want

1

Mark Are you free on Friday?
Linda Yes, I am.
Mark Would you like to [1] ______ together?
Linda I'd love to, but I [2] ______. I'm [3] ______ in the evening.
Mark How about going to the movies at 4 o'clock?
Linda [4] ______. That's a great idea. I'd like to see the new James Bond movie.
Mark Cool. I [5] ______ action movies.

2

Jeff Would you like to play tennis?
Maria No, thanks! I hate playing tennis! And it's going to rain! [6] ______ at the sky!
Jeff OK. Do you [7] ______ to watch a DVD at my house?
Maria [8] ______! Let's do that!

You invite	You reply
Would you like to play tennis?	Yes, I'd love to. No, thanks. I don't like / hate playing, doing, going …
How about going to the movies?	Sure. / Cool. That's a great idea. I'd love to, but I can't / I'm busy.

2 **Pronunciation** **Listen to the intonation of the sentences. Then listen and repeat.**

1 Yes, I'd love to. ↗ 2 I'd love to, but I can't. ↘

3 That's a great idea. ↗ 4 No, thanks. ↘

3 **Listen and put ↗ for accepting and ↘ for rejecting. Then listen and repeat.**

1 ↗ 2 ____ 3 ____ 4 ____ 5 ____ 6 ____

4 **Listen to three conversations. Complete the chart.**

	Would you like to …?	Yes (✓) / No (✗)
1	______________________	________
2	______________________	________
3	______________________	________

5 **Pairwork** **Write dialogues similar to those in exercise 1. Use the ideas in the box. Then practice your dialogues.**

go to the movies listen to music play basketball play computer games surf the Internet watch a DVD watch TV

CD-ROM Workbook p.W18

Grammar

be going to (2)

Think!

Read the sentences and the rule.

Look at the clouds! It's going to rain.

I didn't do my homework. My teacher is going to be angry.

- We use *be going to* to make a prediction based on present evidence.

Rules p.W15

1 Look at the pictures. Complete the sentences with *be going to* and the verbs in the box.

fall make not eat not sleep not win play wash ~~win~~

She 's going to win.

1 He ________ ________ the dog.

2 We ________ ________ the game.

3 He ________ ________ the piano.

4 They ________ ________ pizza.

5 It ________ ________.

6 She ________ ________ a cake.

7 He ________ ________.

Verb + infinitive / *-ing* form

Verb + infinitive		Verb + *-ing* form	
I hope I want I'd like	to write.	I love I enjoy I like I don't mind I prefer I hate	writing.

Think!

Complete the sentences with *going* or *to go*.

- I like [1]________ to the movies.
- I'd like [2]________ to the movies.

Rules p.W15

2 Complete the sentences with the infinitive or the *-ing* form of the verbs.

I like playing (play) volleyball.

I'd like to go (go) to the party this evening.

1 I want ________ (watch) this movie on TV.

2 I don't like ________ (do) homework.

3 I hope ________ (find) a good job one day.

4 Our teacher is very patient and she doesn't mind ________ (repeat) instructions.

5 Pete doesn't enjoy ________ (take) the dog out.

6 Would you like ________ (see) my new car?

3 Complete the text with the infinitive or *-ing* form of the verbs in the box.

find get ~~go~~ live save study travel work

My name's Aya and I'm in my final year at high school. I want to go to college next year. I love [1]________ languages and I want [2]________ a degree in Spanish and German. This summer, I hope [3]________ a job in a café. I want [4]________ some money for college and I don't mind [5]________ hard. When I finish college, I'd love [6]________ around Europe. I'd like [7]________ in Madrid or Berlin for six months.

Finished?

Write sentences about you.

I don't want to … I'd really like to … I hate … I like … I really hope to … I want to …

CD-ROM Workbook pp.W16–W17

What's your star sign?

"I don't believe in horoscopes. I'm Sagittarius and we're sceptical."
Arthur C. Clarke

"What's your star sign?" is a very common question, and one that you probably often use, but do you really know what astrology and the zodiac is all about? The word astrology means the "study of stars" in Greek and it is a very ancient practice. Astrologers study the influence that stars and planets have on people's lives. They believe that the position of the sun, stars, moon, and planets at the time of your birth influences your personality and your future.

You probably know that there are twelve zodiac signs and that they depend on your date of birth. But did you know that astrologers divide the signs into four groups based on the elements fire, earth, air, and water? Aries, Leo, and Sagittarius are in the Fire group. Fire signs are very intense, exciting, and creative. Taurus, Virgo, and Capricorn are Earth signs. People born under these signs are stable and methodical. Gemini, Libra, and Aquarius are in the Air group. Air signs are very friendly and intellectual. Finally, Cancer, Scorpio, and Pisces are Water signs. They are very emotional and intuitive.

Astrologers organize the signs into a circle called the zodiac wheel. People are most compatible with the sign opposite them in the wheel. For example people born under the sign of Cancer are compatible with people born under the sign of Capricorn. Fire–Air and Water–Earth combinations are good. Water–Fire and Earth–Air are bad!

People have very different opinions about astrology. Some people believe strongly in the influence of the stars, but other people think it's all nonsense.

Reading

1 Read the text quickly. Then answer the questions.

1 What zodiac sign are you?
2 What are two characteristics of your sign?

2 Read the text again. Answer the questions.

1 What does astrology mean?
2 How do astrologers divide the zodiac signs?
3 What are the Fire signs?
4 What are the characteristics of the Water signs?
5 Which sign are Leos most compatible with?
6 Do you believe in star signs and horoscopes? Why / Why not?

Listening

3 Listen and choose the correct answers.

1 Emily's birthday is on … .
a April 12th b March 21st c April 20th
2 Emily says she isn't … .
a energetic b patient c stubborn
3 She wants to be a … .
a lawyer b police officer c accountant
4 Star Jones is … .
a an actor b a painter c a TV host
5 Justin Timberlake's star sign is … .
a Sagittarius b Aquarius c Leo

Speaking

4 Pairwork Ask and answer the questions about your future plans.

- Are you going to go to college?
- Are you going to travel?
- What type of job would you like to do?
- Would you like to live a foreign country?

Writing

5 Read Jack's e-mail. Then write an e-mail to a friend. Replace the phrases in bold with information about your future plans.

Hi,

Thanks for your e-mail. You asked me about my future and I have a lot of big ideas! I'm going to **stay at school until I'm eighteen** and then I'd like to **travel around the world for a year**.

After that I hope to go **to college**. I want to **study Media Studies** because I'd like to **work in television**. I want to be **a TV host – they get a lot of money and I'd like to be rich**! What about you? What are you going to do?

Write back soon,

Jack.

CD-ROM Workbook p.W19

4 What will it be like?

1 **Read and listen** **Check (✓) the things that the article talks about.**

a the weather ☐ b school subjects ☐ c food ☐

WALKING THE AMAZON

Ed Stafford, from England, is an explorer. At the moment he is in South America. Why? Because he wants to be the first person to walk along the Amazon River! He hopes that the expedition will help people learn more about the Amazon, the rainforest, and the people who live there. A lot of schools are following his progress.

Here are some questions that students asked at the start of Ed's trip:

How far will Ed walk?

Ed will walk across South America, from Camaná in Peru to the Atlantic coast of Brazil. That's about 6,500 kilometers!

What dangers will there be?

The Amazon can be very dangerous. Ed will meet a lot of wild animals.

What dangerous animals will he see?

He'll see a lot of snakes and he'll see piranha fish and caiman in the river. There are also jaguars in the rainforest, but Ed probably won't see one because they're very rare.

How will he find food?

Ed will have a supply of food. If he finishes the food, he'll have to find food in the rainforest. He'll eat plants and if he's lucky, he'll catch a lot of fish. If he doesn't find food on his journey, he'll get hungry and weak.

What will the weather be like?

The rainforest is in a tropical area, so it'll be very warm and it'll rain a lot. The temperature is usually about 26°C, but it'll be quite cold at night.

2 Comprehension **Answer the questions.**

1 Where is Ed Stafford from?
2 What is his job?
3 Why is he in South America?
4 How far is the journey from Camaná in Peru to the Atlantic coast of Brazil?
5 What kinds of dangerous animals live in the Amazon rainforest?
6 What is the average temperature in the rainforest?

Language focus

3 Read the article again. Then complete the predictions about Ed's journey.

WHAT WILL ED'S AMAZING JOURNEY BE LIKE?

FOOD

1 Food will be a big problem.
2 He ________ plants and fish.

ANIMALS

3 He ________ piranha fish and caiman in the river.
4 He probably ________ a jaguar because they're very rare.

WEATHER

5 It ________ a lot.
6 It ________ quite cold at night.

4 Complete the sentences with phrases from the article.

1 If he finishes the food, ________________.
2 ________________, he'll catch a lot of fish.
3 ________________, he'll get hungry and weak.

5 Focus on you **Read the predictions below. What do you think? Circle the words that match your opinions.**

1 It will be **hot** / **cold** tomorrow.
2 The climate won't get **warmer** / **colder** in the future.
3 **Brazil** / **Italy** will win the next Soccer World Cup.
4 Children won't study **at home** / **at school** in the future.
5 **English** / **Chinese** will be the most important world language in the future.

6 Pairwork **Discuss your choices in exercise 5 with a partner.**

A I think it will be hot tomorrow.
B I agree. / Really? I think it will be cold.

The weather

1 **Match the pictures with the words in the boxes and write sentences. Then listen and repeat.**

~~cloudy~~ foggy raining snowing sunny windy	cold freezing hot ~~mild~~ warm

1 It's cloudy.

2 ____________

3 ____________

4 ____________

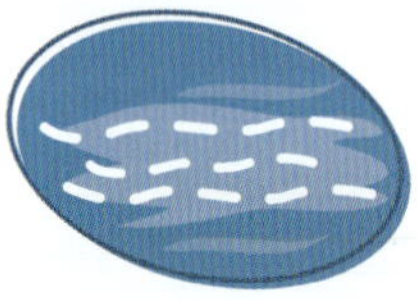
5 ____________

6 ____________

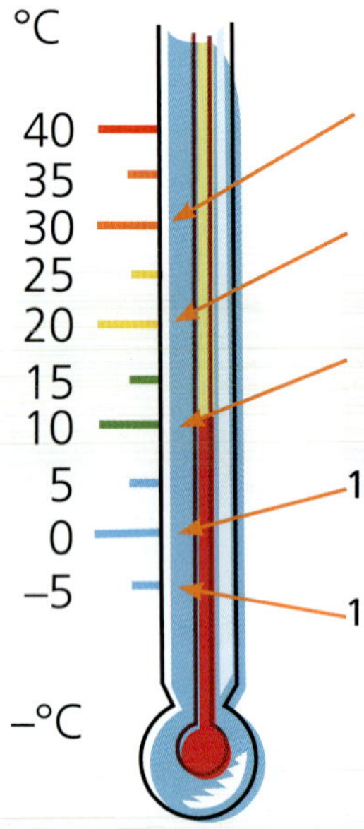

7 ____________

8 ____________

9 It's mild.

10 ____________

11 ____________

2 **Listen to the weather report. What is the weather like in these cities?**

1 London ____________________

2 New York ____________________

3 Sydney ____________________

3 **Pairwork** **Look at the chart. Ask and answer questions about the weather.**

A What's the weather like in Rio?

B It's a hot day. The temperature is 32°C and it's cloudy.

WORLD WEATHER		
RIO DE JANEIRO	32°C	
SAN FRANCISCO	10°C	
PARIS	7°C	
HONG KONG	15°C	
MOSCOW	5°C	
MELBOURNE	30°C	

CD-ROM Workbook p.W22

will: future
Affirmative and negative

Affirmative		
	Full form	Short form
I / you / he / she / it / we / you / they	will win	'll win
Negative		
I / you / he / she / it / we / you / they	will not win	won't win

Think!

- **Read the sentences. Then choose the correct alternative.**
  I think it'll rain this evening.
  It won't rain next week.
- We use *will* or *won't* to talk about future intentions / make future predictions.

Rules p.W20

1 Complete the sentences with *will* or *won't*.

Tim's a great tennis player. I think he will win.

1 Kelly's a terrible driver. She _________ pass her test.
2 Scientists believe the climate _________ get warmer in the future.
3 Al _________ buy a computer. He hates them!
4 I think Liam _________ go to the concert tonight. He loves music.
5 Emma _________ be at the party this evening. She has an exam tomorrow.

2 Make predictions with *will* (✓) and *won't* (✗).

It / be / an exciting vacation. (✓)
It'll be an exciting vacation.

1 We / see / a lot of interesting places. (✗)
2 We / have / time to see everything. (✗)
3 We / eat / Mexican food. (✓)
4 I / speak / English. (✗)
5 I / understand / everything. (✓)

Finished?

Make five predictions about your future. Use *will / won't* and the verbs in the box.

be happy   be rich   have a big house
have a lot of children   live in a different country

When I'm older I think I'll …

will: future
Interrogative and short answers

Interrogative		
Will	I / you / he / she / it we / you / they	win?
Yes,	I / you / he / she / it we / you / they	will.
No,	I / you / he / she / it we / you / they	won't.

Rules p.W20

3 Write questions with *will*. Then answer the questions with your opinions.

It / rain / tonight?
Will it rain tonight? Yes, it will. / No, it won't.

1 you / go / to college?
2 people / live / on the moon in the future?
3 England / win / the next Soccer World Cup?
4 it / snow / in your country this winter?
5 you / be / famous in 2025?

will / be going to

Think!

- **Read the sentences. Then choose the correct alternative.**
  I think it'll rain tomorrow.
  Look at those black clouds! It's going to rain!
- We use [1]*will / be going to* to make predictions based on an opinion.
- We use [2]*will / be going to* to make a prediction based on evidence.

Rules p.W20

4 Complete the sentences with the correct form of *will* or *be going to*.

Careful! You 're going to drop those books!
I hope it 'll be sunny tomorrow.

1 I think Tom _________ like this movie.
2 The score is 5–0! My team _________ win!
3 There's a great smell in the kitchen! We _________ have a nice dinner!
4 Kathy wasn't at school today, but she _________ probably be back tomorrow.
5 The traffic is terrible! We _________ be late!
6 I don't think it _________ snow much this winter.

CD-ROM Workbook p.W22

4 Communication

Making offers

1 **Listen and choose the correct answers. Then listen and repeat.**

1
A Oh no! It's going to rain and I don't have an umbrella!
B Don't worry, **I'll drive you home / I'll give you my umbrella**.
A That's kind of you, but it isn't far. I can walk.
B OK, [1]**I'll get my keys / I'll get you my umbrella**.
A OK. Thanks.

2
A It's hot in here.
B Yes, it is. [2]**I'll open the window / I'll switch on the air conditioning**.
A Great. Thanks.

3
A I'm really hungry!
B There's some cheese in the refrigerator, [3]**I'll make you a sandwich / I'll cut you a piece**.
A Oh yes, please. Thanks.

You offer	You reply
I'll (drive you home)	That's kind of you, but ...
I'll (open the window)	Great. Thanks.
I'll (make you a sandwich)	Oh yes, please. Thanks. / No, thanks.

2 **Pronunciation** **Listen to the pronunciation of *'ll*. Then listen again and repeat.**

I'll make some coffee. I'll help you. I'll cook dinner.

3 **Listen and choose the correct answers.**

1 **I / I'll** make a sandwich for lunch.
2 **I / I'll** cook dinner.
3 **I / I'll** drive.
4 **I / I'll** do the grocery shopping.

4 **Pairwork** **Write dialogues similar to those in exercise 1. Use the ideas in the chart. Then practice your dialogues.**

Problem	Offer ...
can't do homework	to help
thirsty	to make a cup of tea
hot	to open a window
bags are heavy	to carry the bags
no milk	to buy some milk
dinner is ready	to lay the table

A Oh! I can't do my math homework!
B I'll help you if you want.
A Oh, yes, please. Thanks!

CD-ROM Workbook p.W24

First conditional

If clause	Main clause
If it's hot,	we'll have a picnic.
If it rains,	we won't have a picnic.
If it doesn't rain,	we'll go to the beach.
Main clause	***If* clause**
We'll have a picnic	if it's hot.
We won't have a picnic	if it rains.
Will we go to the beach	if it doesn't rain?

Think!

Choose the correct alternative.

- We use the [1]**simple present / *will* + infinitive** in the *If* clause.
- We use the [2]**simple present / *will* + infinitive** in the main clause.

Rules p.W21

1 Complete the sentences with the correct form of the verbs.

If it *snows* (snow) this week, I'll go skiing.
I *won't go out* (not / go out) on Saturday if I have a lot of homework.

1 If it rains tomorrow, we ________ (not go) on the school trip.
2 If we ________ (not leave) now, we'll miss the bus!
3 If Amy gets home late, ________ (her mom / be) angry?
4 I ________ (buy) a CD if I go shopping.
5 If you ________ (not / get up) now, you'll be late for school.
6 If Simon ________ (pass) his exams, he'll be really surprised!

2 Write the sentences.

If / I get money for my birthday / I / buy a camera.
If I get money for my birthday, I'll buy a camera.

1 We / not watch / the movie / if / it / finish late
2 If / they / go / to the U.S. / they / speak / English
3 I / invite / Jake to the party / if / I / see him
4 If / I / have time / I write / to Grandma tonight
5 If you not study / your teacher / be angry
6 I / call Maria / if / she / not be / at school today

3 Complete the sentences with the correct form of the verbs in parentheses.

If it *'s* (be) sunny, we *'ll go* (go) to the beach.

1 If I ________ (finish) my project, Dad ________ (take) me to the baseball game.
2 If you ________ (drink) that coffee now, you ________ (not sleep) tonight!
3 If Mark ________ (play) tennis after school today, he ________ (get) home late.
4 If it ________ (snow) a lot tonight, we ________ (not go) to school tomorrow.
5 If you ________ (eat) all that ice cream, you ________ (feel) sick later!

4 Game! Make first conditional sentences with the verbs in the box. You get one point for each complete correct sentence.

get up go have see snow study win

A Say the first clause of a conditional sentence.
B Complete the sentence and start a new sentence.

A If I win $1,000, …
B If I win $1,000, I'll be very happy! (1 point!) If it snows tomorrow, …

Finished?

Write first conditional sentences which are true for you. Use the ideas in the box.

you don't have any homework this evening
you get a good school report card
you go to the movies on Saturday
you're bored this afternoon

If I don't have any homework this evening, I'll watch TV.

CD-ROM Workbook p.W23

THE ENVIRONMENT – what's in the news?

Scientists believe that the climate is changing and that it will probably be a lot hotter in the future. If that happens, then the world will change in a negative way. Plants won't grow because there won't be much rainwater. A lot of animals will become extinct because they won't have any food and some hot countries will become deserts. But why is the climate changing and what can we do about it? Read on and find out!

Global warming

The Earth produces gases that protect our world. They are called "greenhouse gases" and they surround the planet. Greenhouse gases are good because they help keep the Earth warm. But if we produce too many of these gases they will have a bad effect on the environment because greenhouse gases make the climate hotter.

Am I making things worse?

CO_2 (carbon dioxide) is the main greenhouse gas. We all produce CO_2. You too! Do you use electricity? Does your family have a car? Yes? Then you contribute directly to global warming and you have a "carbon footprint"!

A carbon footprint? What's that?

Your "carbon footprint" is a measure of how much CO_2 you produce in your everyday life. A big carbon footprint means that you produce a lot of CO_2 and that isn't good for the environment. But don't panic – you can reduce it! For example, cycle or walk to school instead of going by car. It won't be the end of the world if we have to change our lifestyles a little, but it probably will be if we don't!

1 Before you read **Discuss the questions with the class.**

1 What is global warming?
2 What is a carbon footprint?

2 Read the text quickly. Then check your answers to exercise 1.

Reading

3 Read the text again. Answer the questions.

1 What do scientists think will happen to the climate in the future?
2 What will happen to some hot countries?
3 Why will a lot of animals become extinct?
4 What do greenhouse gases do?
5 What happens when there are too many greenhouse gases?
6 What does a carbon footprint measure?
7 Do you think your carbon footprint is big or small?

Listening

4 Listen to Emma and Joe talking about the environment. Choose the correct answers.

1 Emma is doing a project for **geography** / **science**.
2 She **answers questions** / **asks Joe the questions** in a questionnaire.
3 Joe **is** / **isn't** interested in the environment.

5 Listen again and complete the questionnaire. How big is Joe's carbon footprint?

Calculate your carbon footprint!

1 How do you get to school?
a by bus / by car — b by bike / on foot
2 How often do you travel by plane?
a once a year or more — b less than once a year
3 Do you have a cell phone?
a yes — b no
4 Do you recycle paper, glass, and aluminum?
a yes — b no
5 Do you use plastic bags for all your shopping?
a yes — b no

Score 1 point for every a.
Total score: ____ / 5
4–5 That's really bad! Your carbon footprint is big! What can you do to reduce it?
2–3 Your carbon footprint is normal, but we're sure you can reduce it!
0–1 Well done! Your carbon footprint is very small!

Speaking

6 Pairwork Ask and answer the questions in the questionnaire. Then calculate your partner's carbon footprint.

7 Discuss with your teacher and the class.

- How can you reduce your carbon footprint?
- Your school has a carbon footprint, too! How can you help to reduce it?

Writing

8 Write a short text about your carbon footprint. Use the questions to help you.

- How big is your carbon footprint?
- What can you do to reduce the size?
- What aspects of your everyday life can't you change?
- What things can you change?
- What will happen if we all make more changes?
- How "green" are you?

CD-ROM Workbook p.W25

B Review

Vocabulary

1 Complete the sentences with personality adjectives.

Our new science teacher is very f<u>riendl</u>y.

1 My brother never helps at home. He is very l________y.
2 Martha always tells me what to do. She is b________y.
3 Charlie is a k________d person. He often helps other people.
4 Carmen doesn't laugh very much. She is quite s________s.
5 Harry and Alex don't think about other people. They are s________h.
6 Jake wants to be rich and famous. He is a________s.

2 Complete the weather report with the correct weather words.

"So, let's take a look at the weather in some of our major cities. In Boston it's very <u>cold</u> and it's [1]________. Temperatures are higher in New York, but it's [2]________. In Seattle it's very [3]________ and [4]________. In San Francisco it's [5]________. Miami is the place to be – it's [6]________ and [7]________."

Grammar

3 Complete sentences 1–6 with *be going to*. Then match them with sentences A–F.

1 Paul <u>isn't going to buy</u> (not buy) the *Avatar* DVD. <u>F</u>
2 Jessica ________ (visit) her aunt and uncle next weekend. ____
3 ________ you ________ (watch) the horror movie on TV tonight? ____
4 We ________ (start) karate lessons next month. ____
5 I ________ (not play) tennis with Peter again! ____
6 ________ Kelly ________ (see) her friends on the weekend? ____

A No, she isn't. She has a test on Monday.
B We want to learn a new sport.
C Yes, I am. It starts at 8 p.m.
D He always wins.
E They live in New York.
F He doesn't like cartoons.

4 Complete the sentences with the correct form of *be going to* and the words in the box.

be sick ~~break the glass~~ have an accident lose the game miss the bus not pass the exam not rain

Be careful. You <u>'re going to break the glass</u>!

1 Hurry up! We ________________.
2 They're playing badly. They ________________.
3 I ate too many cookies. I ________________.
4 The sky is blue. It ________________.
5 You're driving too fast. We ________________.
6 John doesn't know the answers to the questions. He ________________.

5 Choose the correct answers.

I hope (**to go**) / **going** to college.

1 She wants **to get** / **getting** a job in a bank.
2 Jim doesn't mind **washing** / **to wash** the dishes.
3 **I'd like** / **I like** staying in bed late on the weekends.
4 Ray likes **cycling** / **cycle**, but he prefers **running** / **run**.
5 I'd like **to learn** / **learning** Japanese.
6 I hate **do** / **doing** grammar exercises!

6 **Complete the sentences with the correct form of *will* and the verbs in the box.**

~~be~~ do eat enjoy pass see win

Rob is a great soccer player. I think he *'ll be* a champion one day.

1 Mia is coming to the party. We _________ her there.
2 Rachel isn't studying hard. She _________ her test.
3 It's a fantastic movie. You _________ it.
4 You have lots of homework for tomorrow. When _________ you _________ it?
5 She doesn't like vegetables. She _________ carrots.
6 The Lakers are playing very well, but _________ they _________ the NBA Championship?

7 **Complete the sentences with *be going to* or *will*.**

You *'re going to* lose your keys.

1 I think Brazil _________ win the next World Cup.
2 Watch out! You _________ break the lamp.
3 In the future, houses _________ be very different.
4 Look! He _________ take your bike!
5 I think purple _________ be in fashion next season.

8 **Complete the sentences with the correct form of the verbs in parentheses.**

If it *rains* (rain) *we'll stay* (stay) at home.

1 I _________ (help) you if you _________ (not understand).
2 If you _________ (wash) the dishes, I _________ (clean) the living room.
3 What _________ you _________ (study) if you _________ (go) to college?
4 We _________ (celebrate) if you _________ (pass) your exams!
5 If I _________ (get) some money for my birthday, I _________ (buy) a new sweater.
6 If you _________ (not clean) your room, your mom _________ (get) mad.

Got it?

9 **Choose the correct answers.**

Next Saturday, we're going to **have** / **having** a charity day at our school. We're [1]**going to** / **going** organize lots of fun events to make money. The 9th grade students [2]**going** / **are going** to make cookies and sell them in the school. Some boys are going to [3]**play** / **playing** a long basketball game. They hope to [4]**play** / **playing** for twelve hours. We're going to have a barbeque, too. The weather forecast says it will [5]**to be** / **be** cloudy, but it [6]**won't** / **want** rain. Some 8th grade students are going to have a karaoke competition. Some of the teachers want [7]**sing** / **to sing**, too! I'd like [8]**to take** / **taking** part, but I'm very shy and I don't like [9]**sing** / **singing** in public. The 7th grade students [10]**aren't going** / **not going** to talk for 24 hours. If they [11]**will succeed** / **succeed** the teachers [12]**are** / **will be** very happy! Last year we made $850 for charity. This year we hope to [13]**make** / **making** over $1,000.

10 **Answer the questions.**

1 When is the school going to have a charity day?
2 What are the 9th grade students going to do?
3 What will the weather be like?
4 What do some of the teachers want to do?
5 When will the teachers be happy?
6 How much money do they hope to make?

B Culture club

WHAT IS WRONG WITH THE WEATHER?

a

You don't often see people in T-shirts and shorts in the snow – especially not in the summer! But in July 2009 eight centimeters of hail fell on parts of New Jersey. Experts say that it was an extremely unusual incident.

This is only one example of some very unusual weather in the U.S. in the recent years. Last winter there wasn't any snow in the northern ski resorts of New England, but people in the southern states of Arizona and New Mexico saw snow for the first time! In Chicago, Illinois where there is usually a lot of snow in the winter, organizers postponed the annual snow sculpting competition because there wasn't any snow at all.

The Pacific Northwest recorded one of the wettest winters in history. In Seattle, Washington, it rained for 26 days! In California cold weather destroyed crops of lemons and oranges. Economists predict that fruit and vegetable prices will be higher next year as a result.

b

So, what is causing the extreme weather? Some experts say that it's the result of global warming. "We are changing the earth's atmosphere, so we're also changing the climate," says climatologist Tim Rice. "If global warming continues, these unusual weather incidents will become more and more extreme!" Other climatologists don't agree. They say that unusual weather is normal and caused by natural phenomena. "The weather will always be unpredictable," says meteorologist Jan Akken. "That's why it's fun!"

1 Read the magazine article quickly. Where are the places in the photos?

a ______________________ b ______________________

2 Answer the questions.

1 What unusual weather event happened in New Jersey?
2 Why was the weather unusual in New England last summer?
3 Does it often snow in Arizona and New Mexico?
4 Why did organizers postpone the annual snow sculpting contest in Chicago?
5 How many days did it rain continuously in Seattle?
6 Why will fruit and vegetable prices be higher next year?
7 What will happen if global warming continues in Tim Rice's opinion?
8 Why is weather fun in Jan Akken's opinion?

3 Focus on you Write about an extreme weather event (real or imaginary) in your country.

- Describe what happened (when, where ...)
- Did the event cause damage (houses, people, vegetation ...)?
- What caused the event?

My progress

B

Speaking and writing

1 I can talk and write about my future plans. **B1**

I'm going to study English at college.

1 ______
2 ______
3 ______
4 ______
5 ______

Got it? ___ / 5

2 I can identify and describe people's personality. **B1**

He is confident.

1 ______
2 ______
3 ______
4 ______
5 ______

Got it? ___ / 5

3 I can invite people to do things and respond to other people's invitations. **B1**

Are you free on Friday?

1 ______
2 ______
3 ______
4 ______
5 ______

Got it? ___ / 5

4 I can describe weather conditions. **B1**

It's foggy.

1 ______
2 ______
3 ______
4 ______
5 ______

Got it? ___ / 5

5 I can make and respond to offers. **B1**

I'll give you my umbrella.

1 ______
2 ______
3 ______
4 ______
5 ______

Got it? ___ / 5

6 I can talk about my carbon footprint and how I can reduce it. **B1**

I walk to school.

1 ______
2 ______
3 ______
4 ______
5 ______

Got it? ___ / 5

Reading, listening, and writing

			Got it? Yes	I'm not sure	No
7	I can read and understand a text about someone's future plans.	B1	☐	☐	☐
8	I can write an e-mail to a pen friend.	B1	☐	☐	☐
9	I can read and understand a text about an explorer.	B1	☐	☐	☐
10	I can read and understand a text about the environment.	B1	☐	☐	☐

Remember

Vocabulary

1 Complete the sentences with the correct adjectives.

The sun is shining, but it's a c*old* day.

1 Maria wants to get a good job. She's very a________.
2 It's quite c________. I think it's going to rain.
3 I don't like meeting new people. I'm s________.
4 My mom works with old people. She's very k________.
5 I can't see the road! It's really f________ this morning!
6 Mario's l________! He never studies!

2 Add two new words or phrases for each category.

Places in town	Housework	Personality	Weather
1 *hospital*	4 *do the dusting*	7 *stubborn*	10 *windy*
2 ________	5 ________	8 ________	11 ________
3 ________	6 ________	9 ________	12 ________

Grammar

must / mustn't

3 Look at the information. Then write five more rules with *must / mustn't*.

1 *You must sit in the correct seat.*

Brightwell Movie Theater

sit in the correct seat
don't talk during the movie!
don't smoke in the theater
turn off cell phones
don't put your feet on the seats!
take your trash home after the movie

some / any / no / every compounds

4 Complete the compound words with *some*, *any*, *no*, or *every*.

I didn't tell *any*one your secret.

1 I didn't go ________where last weekend.
2 I have ________thing to do. Let's watch a DVD.
3 The city center is very quiet in August. ________one is on vacation.
4 Kelly's uncle lives ________where near here.
5 A "Who was that?"
B "It was ________one from my tennis club."
6 We never do ________thing exciting! We always stay at home.

have to / don't have to

5 Write five more sentences about Natalie's obligations. Use the correct form of *have to*.

At home:		At school:	
load the dishwasher	✓	wear a uniform	✗
take out the trash	✗	stay at school for lunch	✗
clean her room	✓	go to school on Saturday	✓

1 *She has to load the dishwasher.*

6 And you? Write about your obligations. Use the activities in exercise 5.

mustn't / don't have to

7 Choose the correct answers.

You *mustn't* / **don't have to** run in the school corridors!

1 Mom says we **mustn't / don't have to** be late.
2 You **mustn't / don't have to** buy a ticket. The museum is free!
3 I **mustn't / don't have to** cook. My mom always cooks.
4 You **mustn't / don't have to** listen to music when you ride a bike.
5 Sandro's lucky! He **mustn't / doesn't have to** do homework on weekends!
6 Paula **mustn't / doesn't have to** wear jeans to school.

verb + *-ing* form / infinitive

8 **Complete the sentences with the *-ing* or the infinitive form of the verbs in the box.**

buy do listen play study visit ~~watch~~

Kenny wants to watch the movie on HBO.
1 I hope ________ languages at college.
2 Tomas hates ________ soccer.
3 Do you like ________ to music?
4 I'd like ________ Europe when I leave school.
5 Dad wants ________ a new car.
6 ________ housework is boring.

be going to

9 **Complete the text with the correct form of *be going to* and the verbs in parentheses.**

When I leave school. I'm not going to get (not / get) a job immediately. I [1]________ (have) a long vacation first. My friend and I [2]________ (stay) with my uncle in Philadelphia. We [3]________ (travel) around the area and we [4]________ (visit) New York. It [5]________ (be) fantastic! What [6]________ (you / do) when you leave school?

10 **Complete the sentences with *be going to* and the verbs in the box.**

~~be~~ buy clean eat visit watch

It 's going to be a nice day tomorrow.

1 He ________ some bananas.

2 They ________ a DVD.

3 It ________ the fish.

4 She ________ the bathroom.

5 I ________ a capital city.

will

11 **Complete the conversation with the correct form of *will* and the verbs in parentheses.**

Rick What will you do (you / do) when you leave college?
Sasha I think I [1]________ (move) to Hollywood! It's my dream.
Rick Really?
Sasha Yes, I [2]________ (work) at a movie studio, I [3]________ (marry) a famous actor, and we [4]________ (buy) a big house in Beverly Hills.
Rick Yeah, well I [5]________ (not / come) to visit you.
Sasha Why not?
Rick Because you [6]________ (not / be) there, Sasha! It's all in your dreams!

will / be going to

12 **Choose the correct answers.**

Are you going to watch / Will you watch the movie on TV this evening?
1 I think I **'m going to be / 'll be** famous in the future.
2 It's 8:30! You **'re going to be / will be** late!
3 In the future everyone **is going to learn / will learn** to fly.
4 I'm sure that there **isn't going to be / won't be** a free space in the parking lot.
5 What **are you going to do / will you do** when you finish college?

First conditional

13 **Complete the sentences with the correct form of the verbs.**

If it 's (be) snowing tomorrow, we 'll go (go) to the mountains.
1 If I ________ (not have) any homework, I ________ (play) my new computer game.
2 If you ________ (watch) that movie, you ________ (not sleep)!
3 If Mark ________ (play) volleyball tonight, he ________ (eat) dinner late.
4 If it ________ (rain) a lot this morning, we ________ (not go) to the park for a picnic.
5 If you ________ (get up) earlier, you ________ (arrive) at school on time!

5 I've done that!

1 **Read and listen** **Answer the question. Why did Adam call Mike?**

a to talk about exciting activities ☐
b to find out about a new sport ☐
c to discuss a trip to New Zealand ☐

Home Page | Friends Pages | Communities Page | My Photos | Connections | Logout | search

This week's top blogs

I've done that! Zorbing in Tacoma

08/18/10 10:08 a.m. Adam Baker

I've done some cool things in my life: I've been on TV, I've won a competition … and yesterday I tried zorbing! Have you ever heard of zorbing? No? Well, to be honest, I didn't know what it was before last Friday. I called Mike at the Zorbing Center in Tacoma, Washington …

Adam What is zorbing, Mike? I've never heard of it.
Mike It's an exciting new sport. You get into a big plastic ball and roll down a hill.
Adam What?! But that's crazy! And dangerous! Have you ever had an accident in a zorb?
Mike No, I haven't. It isn't dangerous at all. It's great fun!
Adam Did you invent it?
Mike No, I didn't. The idea comes from New Zealand.
Adam Have you ever been to New Zealand?
Mike Yes, I have. Zorbing is very popular with young people there.
Adam Really? Do people need special clothes for zorbing?
Mike No, you can wear a pair of shorts and a T-shirt. Or a swimming costume if you want to try hydro-zorbing.
Adam What's hydro-zorbing?
Mike It's the same as zorbing, but we put some water into the zorb. It's a bit like a washing machine!
Adam What?! You guys are crazy!

Well, I've tried zorbing and it really is fantastic! I want to do other exciting things now, too. I've never done a bungee jump, for example, and I haven't ridden a horse. What about you? Have you ever done anything really exciting? Write and tell me about it!

Reply | add photos | view all | manage | delete

Invite friends | e-mail addresses | add | more

2 Comprehension Answer the questions.

1 What is zorbing?
2 What do people do when they go zorbing?
3 Where does the idea come from?
4 What do people usually wear for zorbing?
5 How is a hydro-zorb different to a normal zorb?
6 Which other sports would Adam like to do?

Language focus

3 Complete what Adam says about his experiences.

"I *'ve tried* zorbing!"
1 "I ______________________ on TV."
2 "I ______________________ a competition."
3 "I ______________________ a bungee jump."
4 "I ______________________ a horse."

4 Listen to Adam and his friend Jessica. Complete their conversation with the words and phrases in the box.

have   Have you ever done   ~~Have you ever tried~~
haven't   've never done   've won

Jessica What did you do yesterday, Adam?
Adam I tried zorbing. It was awesome! *Have you ever tried* it?
Jessica No, I [1]__________. I think it's crazy!
Adam No, it isn't. It's great fun and it's really exciting! [2]__________ anything exciting?
Jessica Yes, I [3]__________. I [4]__________ a karaoke competition.
Adam Wow! Karaoke. I [5]__________ that!

5 Focus on you Check (✓) the things you have done in your life.

I've won a competition.	☐
I've ridden a horse.	☐
I've done karaoke.	☐
I've eaten Korean food.	☐
I've been to a different country.	☐

6 Pairwork Tell your partner about the things you have done in your life.

A I've won a competition, I've done karaoke, and I've tried Korean food.
B I've ridden a horse and I've been to a different country.

Exciting experiences

1 Match the pictures with the experiences. Then listen and repeat.

~~do a parachute jump~~ fly in an airplane go camping go scuba diving meet a famous person ride a roller coaster stay in a hotel travel abroad watch a soccer game

1 *do a parachute jump*

2 Listen and say what the people are doing.

1 They *'re riding a roller coaster*.
2 They ________________.
3 They ________________.
4 They ________________.
5 They ________________.

3 Pairwork Discuss the questions.

1 Which of the activities in exercise 1 are …
- the most / least exciting?
- the most / least dangerous?
- the most / least expensive?

2 Which activities would you like to do? Which would you hate to do?

CD-ROM Workbook p.W28

Present perfect

Affirmative and negative

Subject	*have/has* (not)	Past participle
I / you / we / they	have ('ve) / haven't	visited
he / she / it	has ('s) / hasn't	visited

Think!

Read the sentences. Then choose the correct alternative.

He's visited Peru.

They've won a competition.

- Do we know when he visited Peru? [1]Yes / No
- Do we know when they won a competition? [2]Yes / No

Rules p.W26

Past participles

Regular verbs		
Base form	**Simple past**	**Past participle**
visit	visited	visited
live	lived	lived

Irregular verbs		
Base form	**Simple past**	**Past participle**
win	won	won
sing	sang	sung

See the inside back cover for a list of irregular verbs.

Rules p.W26

1 Complete the sentences with the affirmative (✓) or negative (✗) present perfect form of the verbs in the box.

buy do eat fly meet ~~ride~~ see ~~travel~~

I __'ve ridden__ a motorcycle. (✓)

Tom __hasn't traveled__ around the world. (✗)

1 Lucy ___________ a new skirt for the party. (✓)
2 You ___________ this movie five times! (✓)
3 I ___________ Chinese food before. (✗)
4 Tom ___________ Johnny Depp! (✓)
5 We ___________ in an airplane. (✗)
6 Matt ___________ a bungee jump. (✗)

2 Write sentences in the present perfect.

Nick and Mark / be / to Egypt

Nick and Mark have been to Egypt.

Tim / not travel / abroad

Tim hasn't traveled abroad.

1 Nick and Mark / ride / a camel
2 Tim / not see / a camel
3 Tim / win / a karaoke competition
4 Nick and Mark / not do / karaoke
5 Nick and Tim / watch / a soccer game
6 Mark / not be / to a soccer game

been / gone

Think!

Read the sentences. Then answer the questions.

1 Matt has been to Egypt. He really enjoyed it.
2 Alex has gone to Egypt on vacation.

In sentence 1: Is Matt in Egypt now?

In sentence 2: Is Alex in Egypt now?

Rules p.W27

3 Complete the sentences with *been* or *gone*.

"Where's Sam?"

"He's __gone__ to the teen center."

1 I've ___________ to Paris three times.
2 Dad has ___________ to New York. I hope he buys me a present!
3 We've ___________ to six countries in Europe.
4 Kate isn't here. She's ___________ home.
5 "Where are the boys?" "They have ___________ to baseball practice."

4 Game! In groups talk about the experiences on page 54. Can you remember what everyone has or hasn't done? Write sentences. Who can remember the most in two minutes?

Marcia hasn't been on TV, but she and Luis have met a famous person.

Finished?

Write about your experiences. Use the ideas on page 54.

I haven't been scuba diving.

Booking an activity

1 Read and listen to the dialogue. Complete the booking form. Then listen and repeat.

Receptionist	Hello, Brooklyn Bowl. Can I help you?
Rick	Yes, please. I'd like to book a bowling lane.
Receptionist	Have you been here before?
Rick	Yes, I have.
Receptionist	OK, what's your name, please?
Rick	It's Rick Nelson.
Receptionist	OK, Rick. And when do you want to book the lane for?
Rick	Saturday at 3 o'clock, please.
Receptionist	OK, Saturday at 3 o'clock. How many people are there?
Rick	Three.
Receptionist	So, that'll be $30 for the lane and $4 each for shoe rental. Is that OK?
Rick	Yeah, that's fine.
Receptionist	OK. I've booked that for you.
Rick	That's great. Thanks. Bye.
Receptionist	Bye.

Brooklyn Bowl NYC

Name: ______________

Day and time: ______________

No. of people: ______________

Total price: ______________

You hear	You answer
Can I help you?	Yes, please. I'd like to book a …
Have you been here before?	Yes, I have. / No, I haven't.
When do you want to book (the lane) for?	On (Saturday) at (3 o'clock)
How many people are there?	(Three)

2 Pronunciation /həv/ and /hæv/. Listen to the pronunciation of *have* in the dialogues. Then listen and repeat.

1 A Have you been here before?
B Yes, I have.

2 A Have you booked a bowling lane?
B No, I haven't.

3 Listen to four people making bookings. Match the people with the activities below.

a baseball game   a meal in a restaurant   a movie   a room in a hotel

1 Person 1 ______________
2 Person 2 ______________
3 Person 3 ______________
4 Person 4 ______________

4 Pairwork Read the information below. Then book a lane at the bowling alley.

STAR BOWLING

Opening times: Monday – Sunday 2 p.m. – 2 a.m.

Prices: 1 hour $40 2 hours $60

Under 21s: Saturday 2 p.m. – 8 p.m.
Sunday 2 p.m. – 8 p.m.

CD-ROM Workbook p.W30

Grammar

Present perfect

Interrogative and short answers

Have / Has	Subject	Past participle
Have	I / you / we / they	visited?
Has	he / she / it	visited?

Short answers	
Affirmative	**Negative**
Yes, I / you / we / they **have**.	No, I / you / we / they **haven't**.
Yes, he / she / it **has**.	No, he / she / it **hasn't**.

Rules p. W27

1 Write questions. Then write positive (✓) or negative (✗) short answers.

Has Tom visited Spain. No, he hasn't.
(Tom / visit) Spain? (✗)

1 (she / read) this book? (✓)
2 (Carlos / see) a baseball game? (✓)
3 (they / meet) the President? (✗)
4 (Mr. and Mrs. Brown / buy) that house? (✓)
5 (Ellen / write) a lot of e-mails? (✗)
6 (I / win) the competition? (✗)

ever / never

Think!

Read the sentences. Then complete the rules.

Have you **ever** heard of zorbing?
I've **never** done a bungee jump.

- We use *ever* in [1]**affirmative / interrogative** sentences.
- We use *never* in affirmative sentences with a [2]**negative / positive** meaning.

Rules p. W27

2 Complete the questions. Use the present perfect with *ever*. Then give true answers.

1 Have you ever learned (you / learn) a sport on vacation?
2 __________ (you / stay) at a camp?
3 __________ (you / try) scuba diving?
4 __________ (you / take) your bike on vacation?
5 __________ (you / play) tennis on vacation?
6 __________ (your school / organize) a sports vacation for students?

3 Write two negative sentences for each affirmative sentence below.

Jun has been to Santiago.
Jun hasn't been to Santiago.
Jun has never been to Santiago.

1 We have flown in an airplane.
2 My teacher has met my parents.
3 Nick has run a marathon.
4 I've sung in a play at school.
5 You've been to Hollywood.

Present perfect / Simple past

Think!

Read the sentences. Then answer the questions.

1 **I've flown** in an airplane.
2 I **flew** in an airplane in 2010.

a Which sentence has a specific time reference?
b Which sentence refers to a past action but has no reference to when the action happened?

Rules p. W27

4 Choose the correct answers.

I **'ve bought / bought** a great CD yesterday.
1 We **haven't seen / didn't see** the Eiffel Tower.
2 I **broke / have broken** my leg last year.
3 We **'ve done / did** a hip-hop dance course.
4 **Have you ever eaten / Did you ever eat** Mexican food?
5 I **did / have done** a parachute jump in 2004.

5 Complete the dialogues with the correct form of the verbs or a short answer.

A Have you ever eaten (you / ever / eat) Japanese food?
B Yes, I [1]__________.
A When [2]__________ (you / eat) it?
B I [3]__________ it last year in a sushi restaurant.
A [4]__________ (Su / ever / do) an exciting sport?
B Yes, she [5]__________. She [6]__________ (do) a parachute jump!

Finished?

Write five questions for your partner. Ask about …

food sport travel transportation TV / movies

Have you ever done a bungee jump?

CD-ROM Workbook pp.W28–W29

They've done it!

The Patterson family is back in Chicago after an amazing sabbatical!

Ross Patterson is only thirteen years old, but he's had a lot of exciting experiences. He's visited 29 different countries, he's flown in an airplane 36 times, he's made 47 journeys by boat, and he's traveled a total of 95,000 kilometers!

Ross's incredible journey started fourteen months ago when his parents, Joe and Karen, decided to have a family sabbatical. That means that they stopped their ordinary lives for twelve months and did something completely different! So what did they do? Well, they traveled around the world with Ross and his sister Louise, 17.

During the year, the family traveled to Europe, China, Indonesia, Australia, New Zealand, South America and finally back to the U.S! Things didn't always go well, "Louise lost her passport in Australia, Ross had terrible food poisoning in Indonesia, and we lost contact with Joe for 24 hours when he went canoeing in New Zealand!" says Karen. One of the highlights of the journey was the Great Barrier Reef in Australia. "Dad and I went scuba diving," says Ross, "and it was amazing."

Now the Pattersons are back at home in Chicago, and they are slowly returning to their normal everyday routine. Ross has started his new school and his sister, Louise, has begun a course at college. Joe and Karen have returned to work. "It's great to be back" says Ross, "but I'm already planning my next adventure! This time without Mom and Dad! Next week, I'm going on a school trip to an adventure camp near Toronto. I'm really excited because I've never been to Canada!"

1 Before you read **Read the title of the text and look at the photos. Then discuss the questions.**

1 What do you think the Patterson family has done?
2 What do you think a "sabbatical" is?

Reading

2 **Read the article. Answer the questions.**

1 How many countries has Ross Patterson been to?
2 How many times has he flown in an airplane?
3 Where did the family go on their incredible journey?
4 What problems did they have?
5 What did Ross and his dad do in Australia?
6 Why is Ross excited about the school trip next week?
7 Would you like to travel around the world with your family?
8 Which places in the world would you most like to visit? Why?

Listening

3 **Gemma and Harry are discussing the article about the Patterson family. Listen and decide who has done these things. Write *Gemma* or *Harry*.**

Who ...
1 has never traveled abroad? *Gemma*
2 has been to Canada? ________
3 has flown in a helicopter? ________
4 has visited New York? ________
5 has seen a famous person? ________
6 has tried scuba diving? ________

Speaking

4 **Pairwork** **Read the dialogue. Then ask and answer questions to find out which of the things in the box your partner has done.**

~~do karaoke~~ eat French food fly in an airplane see a famous person stay in a hotel ride a horse ~~visit the U.S.~~ win a competition

A Have you ever done karaoke?
B No, I haven't.
B Have you ever visited the U.S?
A Yes, I have.
B When did you go there?
A I went there in 2008.
B Where did you go?
A I went to Los Angeles.

Writing

5 **Write a short description of three exciting things you have done. (They can be real experiences or you can invent them.) Describe each experience:**

- When did you do it?
- How old were you?
- Who were you with?
- What happened?
- Did you enjoy it?

List two things that you've never done, but that you would like to do in the future. Give your reasons.

CD-ROM Workbook p.W31

6 I haven't finished it yet

1 **Read and listen** **Read the text and find the names of …**

1 four books by Meg Cabot. a _______ b _______ c _______ d _______
2 three books by Anthony Horowitz. a _______ b _______ c _______

WHO SAYS TEENAGERS DON'T READ?

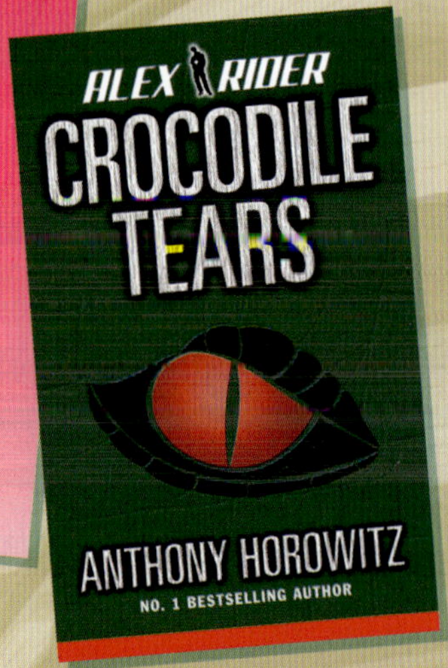

Book sales for teens have increased steadily since the first Harry Potter adventure appeared in 1997. "I started with Harry Potter when I was nine", says Melissa, now fifteen, "and I haven't stopped reading since then." So what type of books are teens reading?

"I love fantasy books and love stories. I've been a big fan of Meg Cabot for two years now. She writes the Princess Diaries books. They're about Mia, a teenage girl from New York who discovers that she is the princess of a small country. There are sixteen books in the series! I've already read the first two books *The Princess Diaries* and *Princess in the Spotlight*. They're awesome! I haven't finished *Princess in Love* yet, but I've already bought *Princess in Waiting*. They've made a movie of the Princess Diaries, but I prefer the books!" ***Jessica, 15***

"I love spy stories. My favorite writer is Anthony Horowitz. His series of books about the teenage spy, Alex Rider, is fantastic. The stories are full of adventure and suspense. I've just bought *Crocodile Tears*, the eighth book in the series. I haven't finished it yet. I've already read all the other Alex Rider stories. *Snakehead* and *Scorpia* are my favorites. I hope Horowitz writes lots more books about this character." ***Ray, 16***

And what about teenagers who don't like reading? "Well, they simply haven't found the right book yet", says librarian Bob Harrison. "There's something for everyone so don't stop looking!"

2 Comprehension **Answer the questions.**

1 How old was Melissa when she started reading Harry Potter books?
2 What are *The Princess Diaries* about?
3 Does Jessica prefer the Princess Diaries books or the movie?
4 What kind of books does Ray like?
5 Who wrote the Alex Rider series of books?
6 What is Bob Harrison's advice to teens who don't like reading?

Language focus

3 Read the article again. Say if these things have happened (✓) or haven't happened yet (✗).

	Book sales for teens have increased steadily since 1997.	✓
1	Jessica has finished *The Princess Diaries* and *Princess in the Spotlight*.	☐
2	Jessica has finished *Princess in Love*.	☐
3	Jessica has bought *Princess in Waiting*.	☐
4	Ray has finished *Crocodile Tears*.	☐
5	Ray has read all the other Alex Rider stories.	☐
6	Anthony Horowitz has written ten Alex Rider books.	☐

4 What does Jessica say about each of the books in the Princess Diaries series? Choose a phrase from the box.

~~I've already read it.~~ I've already read it.
I've already bought it. I haven't finished it yet.

1 I've already read it. 2 ________ 3 ________ 4 ________

5 Focus on you **Look at the titles of the books and write if you have already read them or if you haven't read them yet.**

The Princess Diaries Twilight Harry Potter and the Philosopher's Stone
Snakehead The Lord of the Rings The Golden Compass The Outsiders

I've already read "Harry Potter and the Philosopher's Stone".
I haven't read "The Outsiders" yet.

6 Pairwork **Tell your partner the titles of three books you have already read and three books you haven't read yet.**

I've already read ...
I haven't read ... yet.

6 Vocabulary

Books

1 **Match the book covers with the book types. Then listen and repeat.**

autobiography   biography   detective story / crime story   fantasy story
horror story   love story   ~~science fiction story~~   spy story

1 *science fiction story*

2 **What type of books do these sentences come from? Match the words in the box to the sentences.**

autobiography   biography   detective / crime story   fantasy story
horror story   ~~love story~~   science fiction story   spy story

1 "Sally knew that she was in love with Jack." *love story*
2 "The aliens from planet Nuworld slowly left the space ship." ________________
3 "My earliest memory is of my grandmother." ________________
4 "A secret agent's life isn't always exciting and nobody is really called Bond … James Bond." ________________
5 "Detective Sam Richardson understood murderers." ________________
6 "Vampires are nocturnal creatures." ________________
7 "Tuesday was a good day for Syrus. He killed three large dragons and a monster." ________________
8 "Mozart was born in Austria in 1756." ________________

3 **Pairwork** **Invent the opening sentence of a book. Read the sentence to your partner and ask him / her to guess what type of book it is.**

CD-ROM Workbook p.W34

Present perfect + *yet* and *already*

Think!

Read the sentences. Complete the rules with *yet* and *already*.

Have you read *The Lord of the Rings* yet?
No, I haven't. I haven't read it yet.
Yes, I have. I've already read it.

- 1________ comes before the past particle.
- 2________ comes at the end of the sentence.

Rules p.W32

1 Choose the correct answers.

Have you finished your science project already / yet?

1. Anna hasn't decided which dress to wear **already / yet**.
2. Jonathan has **already / yet** done his homework.
3. Jacob hasn't started his karate lessons **already / yet**.
4. I have **already / yet** sent an e-mail to Mr. Parker.
5. My parents have **already / yet** had breakfast.
6. Have you spoken with Jill **already / yet**?

2 Write the sentences in the correct order.

sent / have / yet / you / the / e-mail?
Have you sent the e-mail yet?

1. movie / started / hasn't / the / yet
2. science / finished / yet / has / Joe / his / project?
3. I've / washed / already / the / dishes
4. the dog / he / for / a walk / yet / taken / has?
5. woken up / they / yet / haven't
6. Mark / finished / has / already / *The Lord of the Rings*

3 Look at Jill's list. Say what she has already done (✓) and what she hasn't done yet (✗).

She's already made the beds.
She hasn't washed the dishes yet.

To do:

Make the beds	(✓)	Do the grocery shopping	(✓)
Wash the dishes	(✗)	Clean the bathroom	(✓)
Feed the cat	(✓)	Clean the living room	(✗)
Water the plants	(✗)	Take out the trash	(✗)

4 Read the e-mail. Choose the correct answers.

Hi, Rob
We're having a fantastic time in Vancouver. We only arrived two days ago, but we've already / yet done lots of things. I've [1]**already / yet** taken lots of photos, but I [2]**haven't / have** put them on my web page yet. We had a picnic in Stanley Park today, but we [3]**haven't / have** been to the Science Museum or the Aquarium yet. I think we'll go there tomorrow. On Saturday, Dad and I are going to a classic motorcycle exhibition. We [4]**haven't / have** already bought the tickets. I can't wait! Has Kate written to you [5]**already / yet?** Is she enjoying her vacation in Hawaii?
Andy

5 Game! Guess three things your partner has already done and three things he / she hasn't done yet today. Write them down.

1 He / She's already made her bed.
2 He / She hasn't eaten lunch yet.

Ask your partner questions to see if your guesses are correct.

A Have you made your bed yet?
B Yes, I've already make my bed. / No, I haven't made my bed yet.

You get one point for each correct guess. The winner is the person with more points.

Finished?

Use the information in exercise 5 to write a paragraph about what your partner has already done or hasn't done yet.

Marta has already made her bed, but she hasn't cleaned her room yet.

CD-ROM Workbook p.W34

6 Communication

Buying presents / souvenirs

1 Julia is in a bookstore. Complete the dialogue with the sentences in the box. Listen and check. Then listen and repeat.

~~Can I help you~~ Here's your change How much does it cost
I'd like to get I'll take it What about

Salesclerk	Good morning. *Can I help you?*
Julia	Yes, please. I'm looking for a present for my dad. [1]_________ him a book.
Salesclerk	Well, what kind of books does he read?
Julia	He loves crime stories.
Salesclerk	Has he read *The Scarpetta Factor* by Patricia Cornwell? It's a bestseller.
Julia	Yes, he has. He's already read it. He loved it.
Salesclerk	[2]_________ *Southern Cross* then? It's by the same writer. I've just finished it. It's great!
Julia	Cool! [3]_________?
Salesclerk	It's \$10, but there's a sale at the moment. There's a 10% discount so that's \$9.
Julia	Great. [4]_________. Here you are.
Salesclerk	[5]_________ and your receipt.
Julia	Thanks.

You hear	You say
Can I help you?	No, thanks. I'm just looking. Yes, please. I'm looking for …
What about …?	No, I don't think so. I think he'd / she'd like that.
There's a sale at the moment.	
There's a 10% discount.	

2 Pronunciation Listen to the pronunciation of the letter *h*. Then listen and repeat.

1 him 2 he 3 has 4 how 5 here

3 Listen to three people buying some souvenirs. Then answer the questions about each person.

	What do they buy?	Who is it for?	How much do they spend?
1			
2			
3			

4 Pairwork Imagine you are buying a present for a family member or a friend. Role-play the scene in the store. Take turns to be the customer and the salesclerk.

CD-ROM Workbook p.W36

Grammar

Present perfect + *just*

Think!

Read the sentences. Then circle the correct alternative.

I've just finished reading it.

She's just started her second book.

- We use *just* in [1]affirmative / negative sentences.
- *just* comes [2]before / after *have* or *has*.

Rules p.W32

1 Complete the dialogues with *just* and the present perfect of the verbs in the box.

finish go have ~~start~~ send

A Do you like the new book by Charlie Higson?
B I'm not sure yet. I 've just started it.

1 A Where's Michael?
B He _________ to school. He left a few minutes ago.

2 A Would you like something to eat?
B No, we _________ lunch.

3 A Does Jill know where to meet us?
B Yes, she does. I _________ her a text message.

4 A Have you done your homework?
B Yes, I _________ it. It was really easy!

2 What has just happened? Use the prompts to write a sentence for each drawing.

clean / her bedroom ~~lose / the game~~ score / a goal see / a movie

They've just lost the game.

1 _________________

2 _________________

3 _________________

Present perfect + *for / since*

Think!

Read the sentences. Then complete the rules with *for* and *since*.

I've studied English for three years.

I've studied Japanese since 2008.

- We use [1]_________ with the length of time.
- We use [2]_________ with the starting point in the past.

Rules p.W33

3 Complete the time expressions with *for* or *since*.

since March
1 _______ a month
2 _______ Sunday
3 _______ two hours
4 _______ yesterday
5 _______ five minutes
6 _______ eight o'clock
7 _______ two weeks

4 Write sentences using the present perfect and *for* or *since*.

He / be / in his room / half an hour.
He's been in his room for half an hour.

1 They / have / that car / 2001
2 She / know / him / six months
3 I / be / here / seven o'clock
4 She / work / in this school / five years
5 Mr. Taylor / live / in London / September
6 She / be / on the phone / two hours

5 Complete the text with *for* or *since*.

Brett Omarson has joined the *Shanghai Tigers* – he is their new guitarist. Brett has lived in New York for five years. He has been friends with the other guys in the band [1]_______ they met three years ago. The *Shanghai Tigers* have been popular [2]_______ over ten years now. They had their first number one in 2005 and they have made four successful CDs [3]_______ then. But they haven't made a new CD [4]_______ 2009. "We've been on tour [5]_______ almost a year, so we haven't had time to write songs and record", says singer Jett Parker. "But this summer we're going back to the studio to make a new album."

Finished?

Write three things that you've just done.

I've just finished exercise 5.

Coffee with Crime

It was ten o'clock and the coffee shop was almost empty.

"So, you've just been abroad," the woman said. "Where were you?"

"I was in Australia," the man answered. "I've only been back since Monday."

"Australia? Wow! I've never been there! What's it like?" she asked.

"I'm not sure," he replied. "I didn't see very much of it."

He stopped. There was a server next to their table. She had a coffee pot in her hand. He waited for her to pour the coffee and then he continued. "I only went there for work," he said.

"What exactly do you do?" asked the woman. "You've never told me."

"That's because it's top secret," he said with a smile, "but it's very exciting. This month I've flown an airplane, done a parachute jump, and met a famous politician!"

"Oh come on! Tell me! I'm your friend!"

"Really, I can't tell you," he insisted.

"You're very mysterious. Is your job dangerous?"

"Yes, it is. I risk my life every day." He replied.

"Do you have a gun?" she asked.

He looked around the room. The only other person in the coffee shop was the server. She was busy and she didn't seem interested in their conversation.

"Yes, I have a gun," he said quietly.

"Have you ever used it? Have you ever killed anyone?" his friend asked with a shocked expression on her face.

"Yes, I have," he said slowly, "I've killed lots of people. The last time was a week ago in Australia."

The server walked quickly out of the room and picked up her cell phone. She called a number and her boss at secret services MI9 answered.

"We have him," she said. "He's just admitted the murder. Send the special forces now!"

"Well done, agent 006," her boss replied.

Reading

1 Read the story and answer the question.

1 Who is agent 006?

2 Answer the questions.

1 When did the man return from Australia?
2 What does the server do when she comes to the table?
3 Why hasn't the man told his friend what work he does?
4 How does the man describe his job?
5 When was the last time the man killed someone?
6 Who does the server call on her cell phone?

Listening

3 Listen to an interview with Lee about his reading habits. Complete the text.

Lee likes reading [1]____________ and [2]____________. He also likes [3]____________ of famous people. His favorite author is Charlie Higson because he likes [4]____________. He hates [5]____________.

4 Listen again and answer the questions.

1 Who is Lee's favorite author?
2 What is his favorite book?
3 How often does Lee read?
4 When does he read?
5 How many books has he read since the beginning of the year?
6 What types of books does he like?
7 What types of books does he hate?
8 What was the last book he bought?

Speaking

5 Pairwork Ask your partner questions about a book he / she has read recently. Complete the questionnaire with his / her answers.

1 What was the last book you read? ____________
2 Who wrote it? ____________
3 What type of book was it? ____________
4 What was the book about? ____________
5 Who were the main characters? ____________
6 What did you like and what didn't you like about the book? ____________
7 Have you read any other books by the author? ____________
8 Choose three words to describe the book: ____________

Writing

6 Write a review of a book you have read. Use the questionnaire in exercise 5 to help you organize your review.

Vocabulary

1 Match the parts of the verbs in A and B.

A	B
1 do	a a soccer game
2 fly	b camping
3 go	c a roller coaster
4 meet	d abroad
5 watch	e a parachute jump
6 stay	f in an airplane
7 ride	g in a hotel
8 travel	h a famous person

2 Recommend a type of book for each reader.

"I like stories about dark nights, empty houses, and strange noises!"
horror story

1 "I want to read about people falling in love."
______

2 "I like reading about criminals and their motives."
______

3 "I love stories about extraterrestrials and alien universes."
______

4 "I want to read about monsters!"
______

5 "I like reading about real people and their lives."
______

6 "I like reading about secret agents."
______

Grammar

3 Complete the postcard. Use the present perfect form of the verbs.

Hello from London!
We're having a great time! We have done (do) a lot of interesting things. We [1]______ (see) the London Eye and we [2]______ (visit) the Science Museum. We [3]______ (walk) everywhere. And we [4]______ (eat) some great food – Thai, Mexican, Italian, and Chinese. We [5]______ (not / have) any bad meals! The stores are cool, too. Mom [6]______ (spend) a lot of money! The weather [7]______ (not be) great, but luckily it [8]______ (not / rain).
See you soon!
Nicky

4 Write questions. Use the present perfect and *ever*. Then write true answers.

your mom / play soccer?
Has your mom ever played soccer?
No, my mom's never played soccer. / Yes, my mom's played soccer.

1 you / visit / New York?
2 you / sing / in a school concert?
3 your dad / be / in a newspaper?
4 Brazil / win / the Soccer World Cup?
5 you / try / a dangerous sport?
6 your English teacher / meet / your parents?

5 Present perfect or simple past? Complete the dialogues.

A Have you ever been (you / ever be) to Australia?
B Yes, I have. I went (go) to Sydney with my family last year.

1 A I can't find my cell phone! [1]______ (you / see) it?
B Yes, I have. It [2]______ (be) under the sofa, but I [3]______ (put) it on the coffee table.

2 A [4]______ (you / ever meet) a famous person?
B Yes, I [5]______. I [6]______ Taylor Swift at a party five years ago.

3 A [7]______ (you / see) the new *Transformers* movie?
B No, I [8]______, but Pete [9]______ (see) it last week.

6 **Look at the list of what a group of students have and haven't done in New York. Write sentences with the present perfect and *yet* / *already*.**

Rodrigo hasn't taken the New York movie tour yet.
Milagros has already seen a Broadway musical.

Rodrigo Take the New York movie tour ✗
Milagros See a Broadway musical ✓
Mizuho Visit the Statue of Liberty ✗
Kana Go to the Metropolitan Museum of Art ✓
Abel Eat at the Hard Rock Cafe in Times Square ✗
Tatsuya Go cycling in Central Park ✓

7 **Choose the correct answers.**

Hi, Katy
We've **moved just** / (**just moved**) into our new apartment in Florida! I've [1]**just** / **yet** finished organizing my books and DVDs, but I haven't put any posters or photos on my walls [2]**just** / **yet**. I've [3]**already** / **yet** met our new neighbors. They are from Bolivia, but they've lived in Florida [4]**for** / **since** five years. The weather [5]**has been** / **was** really hot, but I [6]**haven't been** / **wasn't** to the beach yet. I've already [7]**been** / **gone** downtown and the stores are great.
I miss everybody in Baltimore. I hope you can all come and visit me soon!
Milly

Got it?

8 **Read the text. The crossed out words are incorrect. Replace them with the correct forms.**

Blake High School

Welcome to the Blake High School Book Club.

Blake High School has ~~have~~ had a book club ~~since~~ [1]______ five years. Thirty students have ~~yet~~ [2]______ joined the club this year and the first term hasn't finished ~~just~~ [3]______.
This week's book suggestion is *City of the Beasts* by Isabel Allende.
Isabel Allende has written books ~~since~~ [4]______ over thirty years and she's ~~win~~ [5]______ a lot of prizes. She has ~~wrote~~ [6]______ three books about Alex and Nadia.
City of the Beasts is about a boy called Alex. He has ~~arrive~~ [7]______ in New York to stay with his aunt, an explorer. She ~~have~~ [8]______ decided to take him on a journey to South America. Alex and his aunt meet a girl called Nadia and they travel down the Amazon River. They hear stories about explorers who have ~~went~~ [9]______ into the forest and have ~~ever~~ [10]______ come back.

9 **Answer the questions.**

1 How long has the Blake School Book Club existed?
2 How long has Isabel Allende been a writer?
3 How many students have joined the club this year?
4 How many books has Isabel Allende written about Alex and Nadia?
5 What has Alex's aunt decided to do?
6 What has happened to the explorers?

C Culture club

Alaska Adventure Tours

Home | About us | About Alaska | Tours | Groups | Contact us

▼Alaska – the last frontier!

Alaska – the state of adventure!

**Have you ever climbed a glacier?
Have you ever seen a bear?
Have you ever searched for gold?
Are you looking for fun and adventure? You'll find it in Alaska!
A vacation with Alaska Adventure Tours can change your life!**

More >

Check out our tours!

The Fjords

Arrive in the city of Ketchikan and go by boat to the spectacular Misty Fjords. Here you can see mountains, waterfalls, and wildlife including sea lions, hump back and orca whales, and bald eagles.

More >

Bear watching

Take a boat trip to Anan Creek for bear watching. Watch black and brown bears while they hunt for salmon in the river. More >

Get active!

Take a floatplane and fly to the Gates of the Arctic National Park in the north of Alaska. The Gates of the Arctic National park is a beautiful place with many mountains, valleys, and rivers. In the park you can go hiking, mountain biking, kayaking, or glacier climbing, and of course you must look out for the amazing wildlife – birds, bears, flowers … More >

The Gold Rush

Take a journey into the past. In 1897 a Great Gold Rush started and thousands of people traveled to Alaska to find their fortunes. Today you can re-live the experience! Search for gold in the Klondike river and visit the historic gold rush town of Skagway. More >

Native Alaskan culture

Visit The Alaska Native Heritage Center in Anchorage and discover the history, art, lifestyles, and traditions of Alaska's eleven native cultural groups. Listen to traditional stories and songs and take part in art and dance classes. More >

Your say!

I've been to Alaska with Alaska Adventure Tours three times. I've seen some of the most beautiful places in the world. What are you waiting for?

Nigel Wex, Boston.

Thanks to Alaska Adventure Tours I've traveled by helicopter and floatplane and I've been kayaking and mountain biking! I've seen sea lions, whales, bears, and eagles. Awesome! Just do it!

Rita Li, San Francisco

1 **Read the web page. How many different types of tour does Alaska Adventure Tours organize?**

2 **Answer the questions.**

1 What animals and birds can you see in the Misty Fjords?
2 Why do bears go to Anan Creek?
3 How can you get to the Gates of the Arctic National Park?
4 When did the Alaskan Gold Rush start?
5 How many Native Alaskan cultural groups are there?
6 What activities can you do in The Alaska Native Heritage Center?
7 How many tours has Nigel been on?
8 What exciting things has Rita Li done with Alaska Adventure Tours?

3 **Focus on you** **Write about a popular tourist region in your country. Answer the questions.**

- Where is it?
- What time of year is it popular for tourism?
- What are its main attractions?
- Where can you stay?
- How can you get there and how can you travel around?
- What cultural / leisure / sports activities can you do?

My progress

C

Speaking and writing

1 I can describe what I have or haven't done in my life. **B1**

I've ridden a horse.

1 ______
2 ______
3 ______
4 ______
5 ______

Got it? ___ / 5

2 I can ask my partner about his/her experiences. **B1**

When did you win a competition?

1 ______
2 ______
3 ______
4 ______
5 ______

Got it? ___ / 5

3 I can describe an exciting experience in my life. **B1**

I went to New York when I was ten.

1 ______
2 ______
3 ______
4 ______
5 ______

Got it? ___ / 5

4 I can make a reservation by phone. **B1**

Can I book a bowling lane, please?

1 ______
2 ______
3 ______
4 ______
5 ______

Got it? ___ / 5

5 I can identify different types of books. **B1**

autobiography

1 ______
2 ______
3 ______
4 ______
5 ______

Got it? ___ / 5

6 I can have a conversation in a bookstore. **B1**

I'd like to buy a book.

1 ______
2 ______
3 ______
4 ______
5 ______

Got it? ___ / 5

Reading, listening, and writing

			Got it?	
		Yes	I'm not sure	No
7 I can read and understand a text about a strange sport.	B1	☐	☐	☐
8 I can read and understand a text about teenagers' reading habits.	B1	☐	☐	☐
9 I can read and understand a text about a family's vacation.	B1	☐	☐	☐
10 I can write a book review.	B1	☐	☐	☐

7 What were they doing?

1 Read and listen **Choose the correct answers.**

1 What did the girl steal from Kate?
 a her cell phone b her jacket c her bag

2 What did the boy steal from Andy?
 a his bike b his MP3 player c his sneakers

DON'T BE A VICTIM OF STREET CRIME!

A cell phone, a new bike, or an MP3 player – these are all things you'd probably like to have. But thieves also like to have them and often steal them! Every day young people are the victims of street crime. Read what Kate and Andy say about their experiences and then read our safety tips.

"I was cycling with my friend Jason. We stopped at a café to get something to eat. We left our bikes outside. We didn't lock them, but we sat at the window. While the server was taking our order I looked out the window. A guy was standing near my bike, but he wasn't looking at it. I ordered my food and when I looked out the window again the guy was stealing my bike! I ran out of the café and followed the thief on Jason's bike, but he disappeared. I felt so stupid!"
Andy, 17

"I was waiting at a bus stop with my friend Amy. We saw two girls across the road. They were talking and laughing, but they weren't looking at us. My cell phone rang and I answered it. That was a mistake! The girls crossed the road and one of them asked to use my phone, and I said "No!". She hit me and stole my cell phone! Then the two girls ran away."
Kate, 16

Be safe on the street!

- **Plan your journey and try to travel with others**
- **Keep your possessions out of sight**
- **Put your wallet in an inside jacket or pants pocket**
- **Only use your cell phone when it's safe**
- **Only take what you need when you go out**

2 Comprehension Answer the questions.

1 Where was Kate when the girls stole her phone?
2 How many girls did Kate see?
3 What mistake did Kate make?
4 Why did Andy and Jason stop cycling?
5 Where did they sit in the café?
6 What did Andy do when the guy stole his bike?

Language focus

3 Complete the sentences with information from the text. Then put them in the correct order to tell Andy's story.

_____ We __________ our bikes outside.
_____ I __________ my food and when I __________ out the window again the guy __________ my bike!
_____ While the server __________ our order I __________ out the window.
__1__ I was cycling with my friend Jason.
_____ A guy __________ near my bike, but he __________ at it.
_____ We __________ them, but we __________ at the window.
_____ I __________ of the café and __________ the thief on Jason's bike, but he __________.
_____ We __________ at a café to get something to eat.

4 Listen to Tom's story. Choose the correct answers.

It was seven **fifteen** / **thirty** in the morning.
1 Tom was **walking** / **running** to school.
2 He was carrying his sneakers **and a bag** / **in a bag**.
3 He saw **four** / **five** boys.
4 The boys were standing at **the corner** / **a bus stop**.
5 One of the boys stopped Tom and **pushed** / **hit** him.

5 Focus on you Were you doing these activities at these times yesterday?

8 a.m.	having breakfast
8:30 a.m.	traveling to school
10 a.m.	having an English lesson
1 p.m.	having lunch
3 p.m.	playing soccer
5 p.m.	doing my homework
7 p.m.	watching TV
1 a.m.	sleeping

I was / wasn't having breakfast at 8 a.m. yesterday.

6 Pairwork Tell your partner what activities you were or weren't doing yesterday.

Crime

1 **Match the pictures with the verbs below. Then listen and repeat.**

kidnap someone mug someone ~~murder someone~~ pick someone's pocket rob a bank shoplift steal a painting vandalize a building

1 murder someone

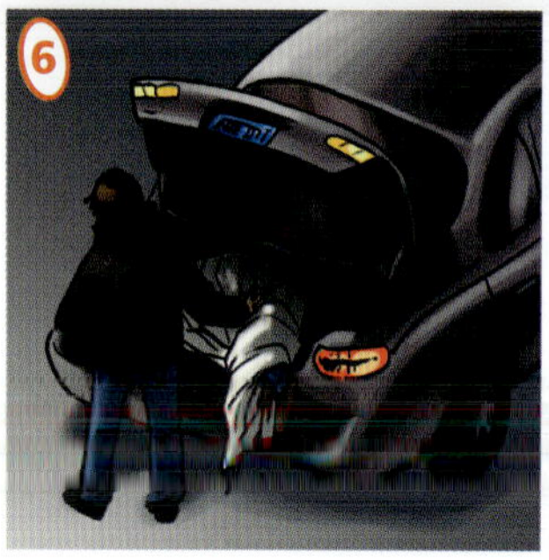

Look!

steal (v) / **theft** (n): to take something from a person without their permission

rob (v) / **robbery** (n): to enter a building and take something from a person by force

2 **Complete the chart with the words in the box. Then listen and repeat.**

kidnapper mugger murderer pickpocket ~~robber~~ shoplifter thief vandal

Crime	Criminal
rob a bank	1 *robber*
vandalize a building	2 ______
steal a painting	3 ______
shoplift	4 ______
mug someone	5 ______
pick someone's pocket	6 ______
murder someone	7 ______
kidnap someone	8 ______

3 **Pairwork** **Put the crimes in the chart in order from the most serious (1) to the least serious (8).**

1 murder someone

CD-ROM Workbook p.W40

Past progressive
Affirmative and negative

Affirmative	Negative
I was playing	I wasn't playing
you were playing	you weren't playing
he / she / it was playing	he / she / it wasn't playing
we / you / they were playing	we / you / they weren't playing

Think!

Read the sentences. Then choose the correct alternative.

We were waiting at the bus stop.
They weren't looking at us.

- We use the past progressive to describe an action in progress in the past / that started in the past and continues in the present.

Rules p.W38

1 Complete the sentences with the past progressive form of the verbs.

Dylan was doing (do) homework all day.
We weren't working (not work) this morning.

1 Max _________ (watch) a horror movie.
2 We _________ (write) e-mails all morning.
3 Troy _________ (not listen) to his teacher.
4 Jim _________ (not wear) jeans yesterday.
5 You _________ (talking) on the phone all evening!
6 I _________ (visit) my grandma this morning.

Past progressive
Interrogative and short answers

Interrogative	Short answers	
	Affirmative	Negative
Was I playing?	Yes, I was.	No, I wasn't.
Were you playing?	Yes, you were.	No, you weren't.
Was he / she / it playing?	Yes, he / she / it was.	No, he / she / it wasn't.
Were we / you / they playing?	Yes, you / we / they were.	No, you / we / they weren't.

Rules p.W38

2 Write questions in the past progressive. Then give true short answers.

you / walk to school / at eight o'clock?
Were you walking to school at eight o'clock?
Yes, I was. / No, I wasn't.

1 you / watch TV / at seven o'clock last night
2 your parents / have dinner / at eight o'clock?
3 the students / do a test / at eleven o'clock?
4 your sister / talk with you on the phone / yesterday afternoon?
5 you / wear sneakers / yesterday?
6 you / sleep / at ten o'clock / last night?

while

Think!

Read the sentences. Then complete the rule.

While I was doing my homework, I was texting my friends.
We were watching TV while Mom was cooking.

- We use _________ to link two simultaneous actions in the past.

Rules p. W39

3 Write sentences. Use the past progressive.

John / play / basketball / while / Peter / take / photos of the game
John was playing basketball while Peter was taking photos of the game.

1 I / not / listen / while / you / speak
2 You / sleep / while / I / watch / the movie
3 While / Susie / walk / she / listen / to music
4 While / they / run / they / chat
5 While / their dad / drive / the children / look / out of the window

Finished?

Say what you were and weren't doing at these times.

three o'clock last Saturday afternoon
five o'clock yesterday afternoon
eight o'clock this morning
at nine o'clock last night

I was walking to school at eight o'clock this morning. I wasn't watching TV.

Communication

Reporting a crime

1 Complete the dialogue with the questions in the box. Listen and check. Then listen and repeat.

~~Can I help you?~~ What did the boys look like? What did they do? What happened? What time did it happen? What was in the bag? What were you doing?

Officer *Can I help you?*
Ian Yes, I want to report a crime.
Officer 1 ______
Ian Some boys stole my bag.
Officer 2 ______
Ian I was walking along Carmine Street when two boys stopped me.
Officer 3 ______
Ian One boy pushed me and the other boy stole my bag. Then they ran away.
Officer 4 ______
Ian It happened at four o'clock this afternoon.
Officer 5 ______
Ian Some books, my wallet, some money, and my keys.
Officer 6 ______
Ian They were fifteen or sixteen. They were wearing jeans and jackets.

You hear	You say
Can I help you?	I'd like to report a crime.
What happened?	A girl / boy / some boys stole my …
Where / When did it happen?	It happened in the park / last night.
What did he / she / they look like?	He / She was tall. / They were tall …
What was he / she / were they wearing?	He / She was wearing / They were wearing

2 Pronunciation Listen to the pronunciation of the sound /ə/ in the sentences. Then listen and repeat.

1 What was in the bag?
2 What were you doing?
3 He was walking along the street.
4 They were wearing jeans.

3 Listen to two people reporting crimes. Complete the crime report forms.

Place: ______
Time: ______
Item(s) stolen: ______
Number of suspects: ______
Description of suspect(s): ______

Place: ______
Time: ______
Item(s) stolen: ______
Number of suspects: ______
Description of suspect(s): ______

4 Pairwork Imagine you are reporting a crime.

A You are reporting a theft. Make notes about the following:
- Where?
- When?
- Stolen items?
- What did the thief / thieves look like?

B You are a police officer. Copy the crime report form from exercise 3. Ask questions and fill in the information.

CD-ROM Workbook p.W42

Past progressive and simple past + *when / while*

Think!

Read the sentences. Then choose the correct alternative.

He was walking to school when some boys stole his sneakers.
Some boys stole his sneakers while he was walking to school.

- We use the [1]**simple past / past progressive** for the interrupting action.
- We use the [2]**simple past / past progressive** for the longer action.

Rules p. W39

1 Match the sentence halves.

1 While I was taking a shower, f
2 Mary fell asleep ___
3 While we were walking to school, ___
4 He was mugging an old lady ___
5 While I was changing money, ___
6 When I saw the boys ___

a when the police officer saw him.
b a robber ran into the bank.
c we saw an accident.
d while she was reading.
e they were vandalizing a phone box.
~~f~~ the doorbell rang.

2 Complete the sentences with your own ideas. Use the past progressive or the simple past.

I was doing my homework when my sister got home.

1 While my best friend was walking to school, ________.
2 ________ when my mom opened the door.
3 While our cat was sleeping on the sofa, ________.
4 ________ when the teacher called my name.
5 ________ while two men were robbing the bank.
6 While he was listening to the radio, ________.

3 Complete the text. Use the past progressive or simple past of the verbs.

call pay put run see steal ~~wait~~

Yesterday, I was in a store and I was waiting to pay. There was a woman and two men in front of me. While the woman [1]________, one of the men [2]________ his hand into her pocket and [3]________ her cell phone. The salesclerk [4]________ him and shouted. While she [5]________ the police, the man [6]________ away.

4 Game! Write a crime story. Use the words in the box to help you. Read your story to the class.

call hear look see vandalize watch

Finished?

Use your imagination to complete these sentences.

When I arrived at Kim's birthday party, ...
While I was traveling to school this morning, ...
While I was doing this exercise, ...

THE HOUND *of The* BASKERVILLES

One morning, Doctor James Mortimer visits detective Sherlock Holmes and his friend Doctor Watson in their rooms at 221B Baker Street, London. Doctor Mortimer tells them about the death of his friend Sir Charles Baskerville. People think Sir Charles's death is part of a 200-year-old family curse. They believe the monstrous Hound of the Baskervilles killed the old man.

Doctor Mortimer got up from his chair. While he was leaving Holmes said, "One more question, Dr Mortimer. You said that before Sir Charles's death some people saw this strange creature."

"Yes, three people saw it," said Mortimer.

"Did anyone see it after the death?"

"No, I don't think so."

"Thank you, Dr. Mortimer. Goodbye."

After Mortimer left us, Holmes sat down in his chair. I knew that he needed to be alone to think about the case. I went out for the day. When I came back Holmes was smoking his pipe and the room was full of smoke.

"What do you think of this case?" I asked him.

"It's hard to say. When Sir Charles died he was running – running for his life. He ran until his heart stopped and he fell dead."

"What was he running from?" I asked.

"That is a difficult question," said Holmes. "I think he was crazy with fear. He didn't know what he was doing. That explains why he ran away from the house instead of towards it. He was running away from help! The next question is: who was he waiting for that night? And why was he waiting outside and not in the house?"

Reading

1 Read the text and answer the questions.

1 Who is Doctor Watson?
2 Where does Sherlock Holmes live?
3 Who is Sir Charles Baskerville?
4 What do people think happened to Sir Charles Baskerville?

2 **Sherlock Holmes is a great detective, but he isn't very good at taking notes! Look at the notes he made about the case and correct the sentences.**

> Three people saw the strange creature after Sir Charles's death.
> *Three people saw the strange creature before Sir Charles's death.*

1 Sir Charles was walking when he died.
2 Sir Charles died because the Hound of the Baskerville killed him.
3 Sir Charles was running towards the house when he died.
4 Sir Charles wasn't afraid when he died.
5 Sir Charles was waiting for someone in the house.

Listening

3 **Detective Clues is investigating the murder of Sir Henry Fielding. Listen to his conversation with a suspect. What was the suspect doing when he last saw Sir Henry?**

4 **Listen again and complete the detective's notes.**

What is the name of the suspect? *Alain Dupont*
1 What is his job? _________
2 When did he see Sir Henry last?
Day: _________ Time: _________
3 Where did he see him? _________
4 Did he speak to Sir Henry? _________
5 What happened while they were talking? _________

5 **There is something strange in the suspect's answers. Can you spot it? Check the answer at the bottom of the page.**

Speaking

6 **Pairwork** **Ask and answer questions about your favorite detective stories.**

- Do you like detective stories?
- Do you have a favorite crime writer?
- Do you watch detective stories on TV?
- What's your favorite TV detective drama?

Writing

7 **Write a short paragraph about your favorite detective from a book, movie, or TV series.**

- What's his / her name?
- Where's he / she from?
- What does he / she look like?
- What type of crimes does he / she investigate?
- Explain what you like in particular about this detective.
  My favorite detective is ...

Exercise 5 Key: He said he was making lunch at 5:30 p.m!

8 I use the Internet to chat

1 **Read and listen** **Complete the chart about Sir Tim Berners-Lee.**

	Sir Tim Berners-Lee
Occupation:	1 ________________
Nationality:	2 ________________
Famous for:	3 ________________

PEOPLE WHO HAVE CHANGED THE WORLD

A lot of people have changed our lives in the last 100 years. Inventors, for example, have created the microchip, a small electronic component which is an important part of today's computers and televisions. Scientists have discovered penicillin, a substance which kills bacteria, and DNA, a molecule that forms the basis of life.

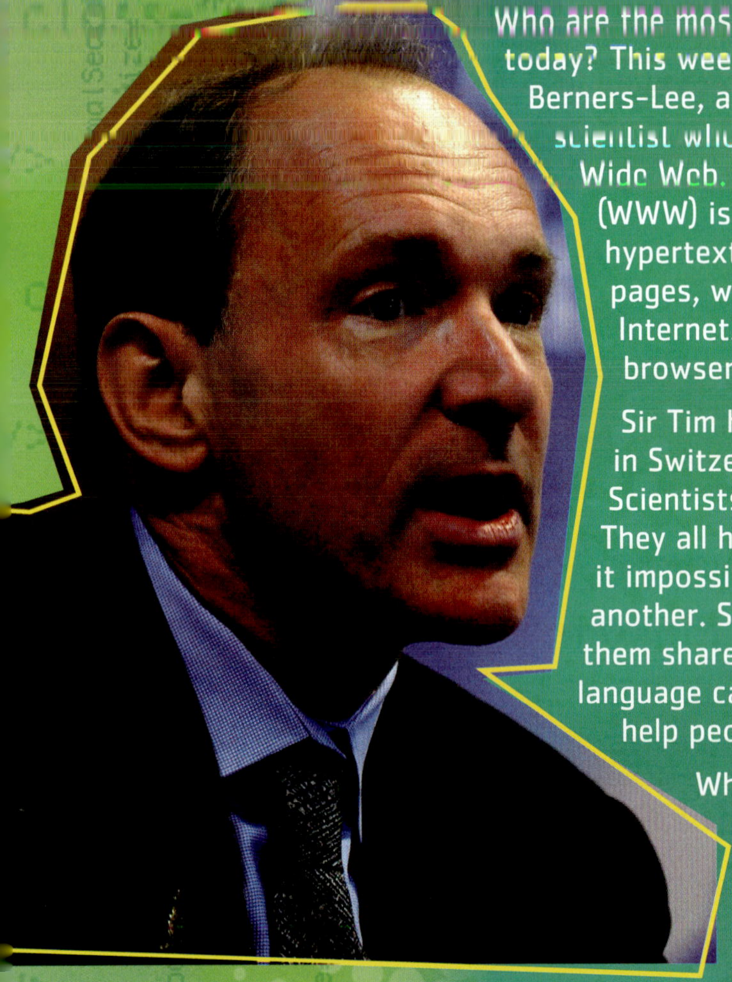

Who are the most important people today? This week we consider Sir Tim Berners-Lee, a British computer scientist who invented the World Wide Web. The World Wide Web (WWW) is a system of linked hypertext documents, or web pages, which is part of the Internet. You can access these pages through a web browser.

Sir Tim had the idea for the Web while he was working in Switzerland at a famous laboratory called CERN. Scientists came from all over the world to work at CERN. They all had different types of computers and they found it impossible to send information from one computer to another. Sir Tim wrote some special programs to help them share information. Eventually he wrote a computer language called HTML (HyperText Markup Language) to help people send and receive computer files.

When Sir Tim connected his computer language to the Internet the World Wide Web was born! Scientists at CERN created the first hypertext website and they put it online on August 6th, 1991. Today there are more than 50 billion websites! People use the Web to buy and sell things, look for information, listen to music, write blogs, show their photos, and much more!

2 Comprehension **Answer the questions.**

1 What examples of scientific discovery are mentioned in the text?
2 When did Sir Tim Berners-Lee have the idea for the World Wide Web?
3 What problem did scientists at CERN have in the past?
4 What computer language did Sir Tim Berners-Lee write?
5 What did the language help people do?
6 When was the first hypertext website put onto the Internet?

Language focus

3 Rewrite the two sentences with one sentence. Start with the words given and find the endings in the text.

The microchip is a small electronic component. It is an important part of today's computers and televisions.
The microchip is a small electronic component which is an important part of today's computers and televisions.

1 Penicillin is a substance. It kills bacteria.
Penicillin is ____________________.
2 DNA is a molecule. It forms the basis of life.
DNA is ____________________.
3 Sir Tim Berners-Lee is a British computer scientist. He invented the World Wide Web.
Sir Tim Berners-Lee is ____________________.
4 The World Wide Web is a computer system. It is part of the Internet.
The World Wide Web is ____________________.

4 Read the article again. Complete the sentences.

Scientists came from all over the world to work at CERN.
1 Sir Tim Berners-Lee wrote some special programs ____________________.
2 He wrote a computer language called HTML ____________________.
3 Today people use the Web ____________________.

5 Focus on you **Why do you do these things? Underline the most important reasons.**

I go to school
a to study | b to meet friends | c to see the teachers

I use the Internet
a to do homework | b to chat | c to send e-mails

I watch TV
a to relax | b to get the news | c to learn new things

I meet friends
a to play sport | b to chat | c to listen to music

I save money
a to buy sweets | b to buy clothes | c to buy presents

6 Pairwork **Discuss your answers to exercise 5.**

A I go to school to study.
B So do I. / Really? I go to school to meet my friends.

Human achievement

1 **Label the people with the words in the box. Then listen and repeat.**

architect   artist   composer   explorer   ~~inventor~~   politician   scientist   writer

1 inventor

2 **Match the people with the verbs.**

1 inventor — d	a travel / explore
2 scientist	b negotiate / debate
3 artist	c write
4 composer	d invent
5 explorer	e paint / draw
6 writer	f discover
7 architect	g compose music
8 politician	h build / design

3 **Match the famous people to their professions and achievements. Then write two sentences about each person.**

Shakespeare	explorer	first U.S. President
Marie Curie	politician	*Guernica* (1937)
Christopher Columbus	artist	the theory of radioactivity
George Washington	writer	*Romeo and Juliet*
Picasso	scientist	the Americas

Shakespeare was a famous writer. He wrote "Romeo and Juliet".

4 **Pairwork** **Think of a famous person for each category in exercise 1. Find out if your partner knows why they are famous.**

A Who was Beethoven?

B He was a German composer.

Grammar

8

Relative pronouns: *who* / *which* / *that*

People
The book is about a boy. He makes friends with a dog.
The book is about boy ***who*** / ***that*** makes friends with a dog.
Things
Stephenie Meyer writes books. The books are very exciting.
Stephenie Meyer writes books ***which*** / ***that*** are very exciting.

Think!

Read the sentences. Then complete the rules with ***who*** and ***which***.

Marie Curie was the scientist who discovered radium.

Radium is an element which is radioactive.

- The relative pronoun [1]________ refers to people.
- The relative pronoun [2]________ refers to animals or things.

Rules p.W44

1 Circle the correct answers.

Gustave Eiffel was the man who / that designed the Eiffel Tower.

1 Isaac Newton was the man **who / which** described the law of gravity.
2 Penicillin is a drug **which / who** kills bacteria.
3 A composer is a person **who / which** writes music.
4 The airplane was an invention **who / which** changed the world.
5 Marconi was the person **which / who** invented the radio.
6 The Internet is a network **who / which** connects computers.

2 Complete the definitions with *who* or *which* and a phrase from the box.

contains genetic code | created the miniskirt | ~~debate and create laws~~ | discovered penicillin | created Mickey Mouse | stores and plays music files

Politicians are people who debate and make laws.

1 Walt Disney is the man ______________.
2 DNA is the molecule ______________.
3 Alexander Fleming is the person ______________.
4 An MP3 player is an electronic device ______________.
5 Mary Quant is the fashion designer ______________.

3 Join the sentences together. Rewrite them with *who*, *which*, or *that*.

Charlie Chaplin was an actor. He appeared in silent movies.

Charlie Chaplin was an actor who appeared in silent movies.

1 Michelangelo was an artist. He lived in the Renaissance period.
____
2 An oven is an electronic device. It cooks food.
____
3 Magellan was an explorer. He came from Portugal.
____
4 A dishwasher is a machine. It cleans plates.
____
5 This is the book. My sister read it last year.
____

4 Game! Take turns to describe the people or things in the box. Guess who or what your partner is describing.

~~an airplane~~ | a dog | a DVD player | an iron | a love story | a salesclerk | a shoplifter | a student | a teacher | a vandal

A It is a machine that flies in the sky. You can sit in it and travel to other countries.
B An airplane!

Finished?

Write five more definitions for people and things.

A doctor is a person who works in a hospital.
A novel is a book which tells a story.

CD-ROM Workbook p.W46

8 Communication

Discussing what things are for

1 **Match the dialogues with the pictures. Then listen and repeat.**

a 

b 

c 

1 A What's this gadget?
B It's a book light.
A What's it for?
B It's for reading in the dark. You attach it to a book and you use it to read in bed or in the car.

2 A What's this?
B It's an external hard drive.
A What's it for?
B It's for storing information from your computer. You use it to keep back-up copies of your computer files.

3 A What are these?
B They're aqua globes.
A What are they for?
B They're for watering your plants. You put water in them and then you put them in your plant pots.

You hear	You answer
What's this / are these?	It's a / an … . / They're … .
What's it for?	It's for (reading). / They're for (watering your plants).
What are they for?	You use it / them to (read / water your plants).

2 **Pronunciation** **Listen to the pronunciation of the sound /ð/. Then listen and repeat.**

1 this
2 these
3 they
4 then
5 them

3 **Listen to three conversations. Complete the notes about the gadgets.**

1 A waterproof ________ Use: for ________ in the shower!
2 A speaker ________ Use: for ________ calls in the car.
3 An MP3 ________ Use: for ________ and listening to music.

4 **Pairwork** **Ask and answer questions about these gadgets.**

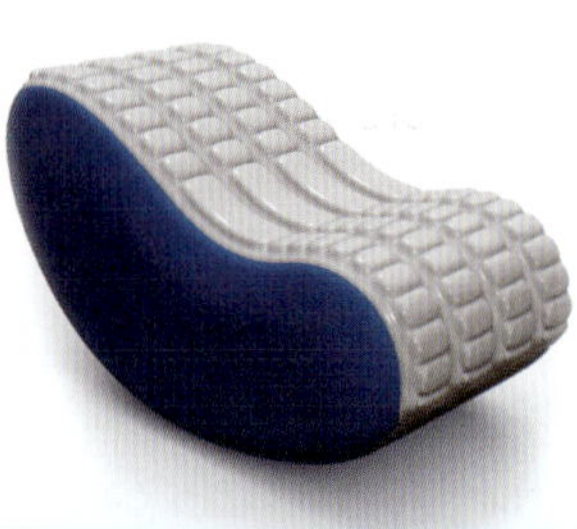

Exercise bean
Use: exercise - keep fit and work out at home!

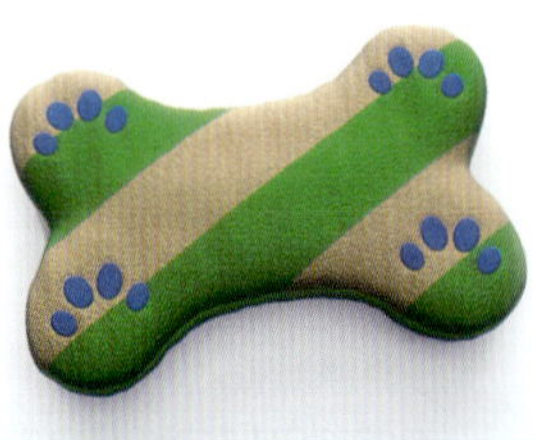

Talking bone
Use: keep your dog happy – record your voice and talk to your dog!

Jumbo Remote Control
Use: control your TV and other electronic devices – controls all your electronic devices!

Digital recorder
Use: record your voice and conversations – no need to take notes in class!

CD-ROM Workbook p.W48

The infinitive of purpose

Think!

Read the sentences. Then check (✓) the correct answers.

He went to London **to study English**.
I surfed the Internet **to find information about New York**.

1 What is the function of the **bold** phrases?
   a to describe an event ☐
   b to describe a reason or purpose ☐
2 What form does the verb in the phrases take?
   a the infinitive with *to* ☐
   b the infinitive without *to* ☐

Rules p.W44

1 Match the sentence halves.

1 She went into the store
2 Marcus called Maria
3 I went to the library
4 Thomas called the police
5 We bought some cake
6 Valeria went online

a to report a crime.
b to celebrate Larry's birthday.
c to buy a newspaper.
d to check her e-mails.
e to borrow a book.
f to invite her to the theater.

2 Look at the pictures and complete the sentences.

She got a pen *to write a letter*.

1 He went to the sports center ____________.

2 Arthur cut some bread ____________.

3 They went into the store ____________.

4 Yuki went to her bedroom ____________.

5 Vitor got his MP3 player ____________.

Which one ...? / Which ones ...?

Singular
A These T-shirts are cool!
B **Which one** do you like best?
A I like the blue **one**.
Plural
A Help me choose some shoes. **Which ones** do you prefer?
B I prefer the brown **ones**.

Think!

Read the sentences. Then choose the correct alternative.

I like the blue T-shirt. I don't like the red **one**.
These DVDs are great. Those **ones** are boring.

- You can use [1]*one / ones* to avoid repeating [2]an adjective / a countable noun.

Rules p.W45

3 Rewrite the sentences. Use *one* or *ones*.

Which T-shirt is more expensive? The red T-shirt or the blue T-shirt?
Which T-shirt is more expensive? The red one or the blue one?

1 There are some CDs on the table. Which CDs are yours?
2 Which sandwich do you want? The sandwich with cheese or the sandwich with chicken?
3 A Look at these cell phones. Which phone do you prefer?
   B I prefer the black phone. It's smaller.
4 A Which shoes do you like? The red shoes or the brown shoes?
   B I like the brown shoes.
5 A Which of those boys is your brother?
   B The tallest boy.
6 Those DVDs aren't as good as these DVDs.

Finished?

Look for three examples of these things in your book. Say which one you prefer.

animals   boys   cities   gadgets   girls

There are photos of cities on pages 28, 48, and 63. I prefer the one on page 63.

THE GENIUS WHO INVENTED TELEVISION

John Logie Baird was a Scottish engineer and inventor. He was born on August 14th, 1888. During his life Baird invented a lot of different things, but he is famous because he was the man who invented one of the most popular electronic devices in the world – the television.

As a child Baird was very interested in electricity and technology. As a teenager, he changed the lights in his family's house from gas lamps to electric lights! He also created a small phone network which connected his bedroom with his friends' bedrooms in houses across the street!

After World War I, Baird moved to England to start work on the development of television. A lot of scientists were doing similar work, but in October 1925 Baird was the first person to produce and transmit a television image that moved. He also invented the first working television and demonstrated his television to 50 scientists in London on January 26th 1926. A year later he formed the Baird Television Development Company Ltd. (BTDC). The BTDC was the company which transmitted the first transatlantic television signal from London to New York.

John Logie Baird died on June 14th 1946, but his invention lives on. Today television is a form of entertainment which is popular all over the world. People watch TV in their free time to relax and to learn about the world.

Reading

1 Read the text quickly. Answer the question.

1 What was John Logie Baird's most important achievement?

2 Answer the questions.

1 What nationality was John Logie Baird?
2 When was he born?
3 What was he interested in as a child?
4 Why did he move to England after World War I?
5 When did he give the first demonstration of his television?
6 Where did his demonstration of television happen?
7 Why was John Logie Baird's company important?
8 When did John Logie Baird die?

Listening

3 **Ruth and Chris are discussing the objects below. Which ones do they prefer? Listen and write *R* (Ruth) or *C* (Chris) next to each object.**

1a

1b

2a

2b

3a
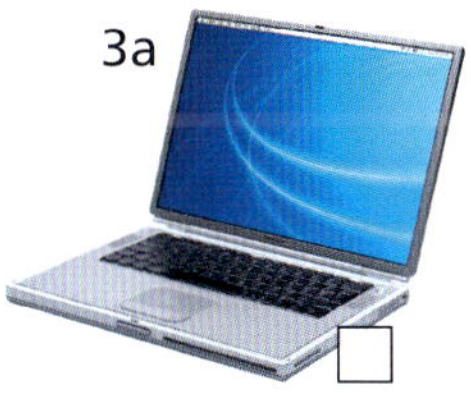
3b
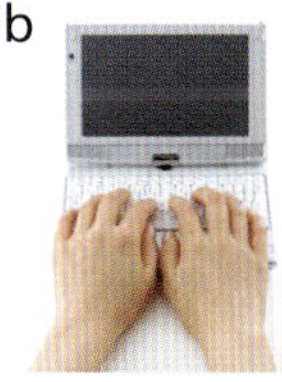
4a

4b

Speaking

4 **Pairwork** **Look at the objects in exercise 3 again. Discuss which ones you prefer.**

A What do you think of the TVs? Which one do you prefer?
B I like the modern one best, of course! It has … .
A I prefer that one, too. The other one is … . / Really? I prefer the old-fashioned one. It has … .

Writing

5 **Read the factfile about Alexander Graham Bell. Then complete the text.**

Alexander Graham Bell was a Scottish *scientist* and [1]_________. He was born on [2]_________. Bell is famous because he was one of the people [3]_________ telephone. He created his version of the telephone in [4]_________. He died on [5]_________. Today the [6]_________ is one of the most common electronic devices in the world. People use them for business and to stay in contact with their family and friends.

Alexander Graham Bell
Nationality: Scottish
Occupation: scientist and inventor
Born: March 3rd, 1847
Died: August 2nd, 1922
Inventions: 1875 - the telephone

6 **Write a paragraph about one of the people in the factfiles below. Say:**

- who he is / was and where he was born
- why he is famous and what he invented
- how popular the invention is today
- what people use it for
- if you have one and how important it is to your life

László Bíró
Nationality: Hungarian
Occupation: journalist and inventor
Born: September 29th, 1899
Died: October 24th, 1985
Invention: 1931 - the ball point pen (biro)

Martin Cooper
Nationality: American
Occupation: engineer and inventor
Born: December 26th, 1928
Invention: 1973 - the cell phone

CD-ROM Workbook p.W49

D Review

Vocabulary

1 Complete the newspaper article with the words in the box.

kidnapped kidnappers mugged muggers ~~murder~~ murderer pickpockets robbed robbers shoplifters stole thief vandals vandalized

Police have started a murder inquiry after the death of William Travis. They believe that Mr. Travis knew his [1]_________.

Two men [2]_________ the City bank yesterday. The [3]_________ escaped with $40,000.

On Friday two men [4]_________ an old woman's dog. The [5]_________ want $1000,000 for its safe return.

A [6]_________ broke into the Webber Art Gallery on Friday night and [7]_________ five paintings.

Two teenagers [8]_________ Ellen Clover at the bus stop in West Street yesterday. The [9]_________ escaped with her purse.

Some boys [10]_________ a park play area in the city last night. The [11]_________ sprayed graffiti and destroyed the park benches.

Angry store owners in Langley Mall have put security cameras in their stores to help catch [12]_________. Security guards at the mall also advise customers to watch out for [13]_________.

2 Answer the questions.

WHAT DO YOU CALL A PERSON WHO ...?

1. writes music — a composer
2. paints and draws pictures — an a_________
3. writes novels and plays — a w_________
4. travels through unknown territories — an e_________
5. debates and votes on new laws — a p_________
6. creates new machines — an i_________
7. designs buildings — an a_________
8. studies the natural world and makes new discoveries — a s_________

Grammar

3 Complete the dialogues with the past progressive form of the verbs and short answers.

a

Police What were you doing (you / do) at 8 a.m. yesterday?

Suspect 1 I was at home. My wife [1]_________ (cook) breakfast and my children [2]_________ (get) ready for school. I [3]_________ (watch TV).

b

Police [4]_________ (you / stand) outside the bank at 8 a.m?

Suspect 2 Yes, I [5]_________ but I [6]_________ (not / wait) for the bank to open. I [7]_________ (wait) for the bus.

c

Police [8]_________ (you / sit) in a car near the bank at 8 a.m?

Suspect 3 No, I [9]_________! I was with two friends. We [10]_________ (drive) to work.

4 Complete the dialogue with the past progressive or the simple past of the verbs.

A I saw (see) something very exciting yesterday.

B What [1]_________ (you / see)?

A Well I [2]_________ (do) my homework when I [3]_________ (hear) a noise. I went to the window and I saw two men. They [4]_________ (stand) in the Liptons' back yard!

B What [5]_________ (they do) when you [6]_________ (see) them?

A They [7]_________ (try) to open a window!

B Really? What happened then?

A While they [8]_________(open) the window, the house alarm [9]_________ (start) to ring and they ran away! I called the police, but while I [10]_________ (report) the crime a police car [11]_________ (arrive). The thieves [12]_________ (run) down the street when the police [13]_________ (stop) them!

5 Rewrite the sentences with *who* or *which*.

Gemma is the girl that won the competition.
Gemma is the girl who won the competition.

1 The man that answered the phone was my dad.
____
2 Marconi is the man that invented the radio.
____
3 A sushi bar is a restaurant that serves Japanese food.
____
4 The salesclerk that served us was very nice.
____
5 The red car that is in front of the house is my mom's.
____
6 *Up* is a movie that was popular in 2009.
____

6 Combine the sentences. Use *who* or *which / that*.

Magellan was an explorer. He traveled to the Americas.
Magellan was an explorer who traveled to the Americas.

1 *Ring of Life* is a book about an old ring. The ring has magical powers.
2 Andy Warhol was an American painter. He was an important pop artist.
3 *Alien Attack* is a movie about an alien space ship. It attacks planet Earth.
4 J.K. Rowling is a writer. She is famous for writing the Harry Potter books.

7 Choose the correct answers.

You use a bottle-opener **for** / **to** open bottles.

1 A USB pen is **for** / **to** storing information from your computer.
2 He went into the store **for to** / **to** buy some bread.
3 "Which of those girls is your sister?" "The **one** / **ones** with red hair."
4 I called Jack **for** / **to** say Happy Birthday.
5 Those clothes are less expensive than these **one** / **ones**.
6 Which **one** / **ones** do you prefer? The red top or the blue top?
7 He went to the library **to** / **for** find a book.

Got it?

8 Complete the text with the simple past or the past progressive form of the verbs and choose the correct relative pronouns.

Daisy Richardson, is a 15-year-old girl **who** / **which** survived when a car crashed into her bedroom.

Daisy was sleeping (sleep) when the car [1]_______________ (crash) through her bedroom wall. The car [2]_______________ (push) a wardrobe onto her bed [3]**who** / **which** saved her! The police arrested the man [4]**who** / **which** caused the accident, 23-year-old Jason Edwards.

Mr. Edwards [5]_______________ (driving) home when the accident [6]_______________ (happen). "It [7]_______________ (rain) and I [8]_______________ (lose) control of the car. Luckily I [9]_______________ (not drive) very fast," he said. The police, however, think that Mr. Edwards [10]_______________ (use) his cell phone at the time of the accident and that he [11]_______________ (not concentrate) on the road. They believe he tried to stop suddenly at a traffic light [12]**who** / **which** is outside the Richardsons' house and lost control. They would like anyone [13]**who** / **which** saw the accident to contact them [14]**for** / **to** help them with their inquiries.

9 Answer the questions.

1 What was Daisy doing when the car crashed into her house?
2 Who is Jason Edwards?
3 What does Mr. Edwards think happened?
4 What do the police think Mr. Edwards was doing at the time of the accident?
5 How do the police think that Mr. Edwards lost control?
6 What must people who saw the accident do?

ORDINARY PEOPLE, EXTRAORDINARY ACTIONS

CNN Heroes

In 2007 the American TV channel CNN created a special competition to honor ordinary people who do extraordinary things to help others. They asked people to nominate and vote for their local heroes. In the first year CNN received more than 7,000 nominations from people in over 80 different countries. Today the competition is an annual event. Here are two of the recent winners.

Wesley Autrey

Wesley Autrey was waiting for a train in a New York subway station when a young man fell onto the train tracks. Autrey immediately jumped onto the tracks to help him. He was trying to move the man when he heard a train coming. Autrey lay on top of the young man to protect him between the train tracks. Amazingly, the train passed over them and both men survived.

Derrick Tabb

Derrick Tabb works hard to keep young people away from crime in New Orleans, the city which has the highest murder rate in the U.S. He runs a program called *The Roots of Music* which offers free music lessons to more than 100 students between the ages of nine and fourteen. The students meet from 4 p.m.–7 p.m. every weekday. They practice their music, do their homework, and have a hot meal before they go home.

The Roots of Music is a very popular program and more than 400 young people are waiting to join. Every day the students learn something new, so they want to come back every day. One of the young musicians says "Before, I was always in trouble. Now, when I come here, I'm learning how to play the drums, be disciplined, and work hard".

The students work hard on the program, but interestingly they also work harder in school – 85% of the children who take part in the program have better grades in class. Derrick Tabb believes that music can give children a better future and it seems that his program is working.

1 Before you read **Read the text quickly. Check (✓) the correct ending to the sentence.**

The article is about people … .

- a who have an extraordinary talent ☐
- b who helped other people in extraordinary ways ☐
- c who have extraordinary lives ☐

2 Answer the questions.

1 When did CNN create a special competition?
2 Why did CNN create the competition?
3 What happened while Wesley Autrey was waiting for a train?
4 What did Wesley Autrey do?
5 How does Derrick Tabb try to keep young people away from crime?
6 How often do the students meet and what do they do?
7 Is *The Roots of Music* program popular?
8 How does the program help some young people in other areas of their lives?

3 Focus on you **Write about a person you know who does a lot to help others. Include the following information …**

- who he / she is
- why he / she is a hero
- what he / she does to help others

My progress

D

Speaking and writing

1 I can identify different types of crime. **B1**

kidnap someone

1 ______
2 ______
3 ______
4 ______
5 ______

Got it? ___ / 5

2 I can ask and answer questions about my favorite detective stories. **B1**

I like detective stories.

1 ______
2 ______
3 ______
4 ______
5 ______

Got it? ___ / 5

3 I can describe my favorite detective from a book, a movie, or a TV series. **B1**

My favorite detective is Hercule Poirot.

1 ______
2 ______
3 ______
4 ______
5 ______

Got it? ___ / 5

4 I can identify different occupations. **B1**

architect

1 ______
2 ______
3 ______
4 ______
5 ______

Got it? ___ / 5

5 I can write about famous people and their achievements. **B1**

Gustave Eiffel was the man who designed the Eiffel Tower.

1 ______
2 ______
3 ______
4 ______
5 ______

Got it? ___ / 5

6 I can write a factfile about a famous inventor. **B1**

Albert Einstein was born in Germany.

1 ______
2 ______
3 ______
4 ______
5 ______

Got it? ___ / 5

Reading, listening, and writing

			Got it? Yes	I'm not sure	No
7	I can read an article about street crime.	**B1**	☐	☐	☐
8	I can read and understand a story about Sherlock Holmes.	**B1**	☐	☐	☐
9	I can read and understand articles about different inventors.	**B1**	☐	☐	☐
10	I can read and understand an article about an extraordinary person.	**B1**	☐	☐	☐

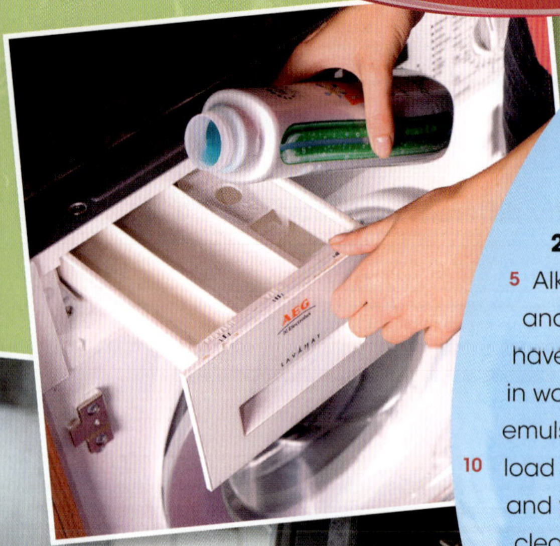

1 Chemicals in everyday life

Everyone has to wash their clothes, wash the dishes, and clean the bath. Most of us use cleaning products with alkalis or acids in them to do these chores. But do we know what alkalis and acids are or how they work?

2 ________________

Alkalis are chemicals and they are everywhere: in soap, dishwasher tablets, and washing powder. But how do they clean our dirty clothes and plates? Alkalis have two parts: one part loves water, the other part loves dirt. The two parts react in water and the water particles get bigger. This produces a new liquid called an emulsion. The emulsion attracts the dirt from your clothes or dishes. So when you load the washing machine and switch it on, the detergent causes that reaction and you get clean clothes. However, you don't have to mix an alkali in water to clean dirt. Oven cleaners, for example, contain a very strong alkali called sodium hydroxide. This reacts with the dirt in the oven and dissolves it.

3 ________________

Acids are also chemicals and they contain the gas hydrogen. There are different kinds of acids. Fruits contain citric acid, vinegar is an acid, fizzy drinks are also acids. Some household cleaning products use a mixture of a strong acid and water. Toilet cleaners contain strong acids, but they have to be mixed with water. This mixture of acid and water kills germs.

4 ________________

Acids often sting when you touch them and they react strongly when they combine with metal. Acids are dangerous and they can burn you. You must read the label on a product carefully before you use it. When you clean something with an acid, you must wear gloves. If acid touches your skin, you must wash it off immediately.

5 ________________

No one likes damaging the environment. Cleaning products with chemicals damage the environment and they are also bad for everyone's health. Nowadays many people prefer using environmentally-friendly products with plant-based ingredients to clean their house or more natural products like lemon juice and vinegar. Some people mix a cooking powder called bicarbonate of soda with water. This makes a paste and it cleans very well.

Did you know?

Bee stings are acid. Don't use lemon juice! Use an alkali, for example bicarbonate of soda!
Wasp stings are alkaline. Use an acid, for example lemon juice!

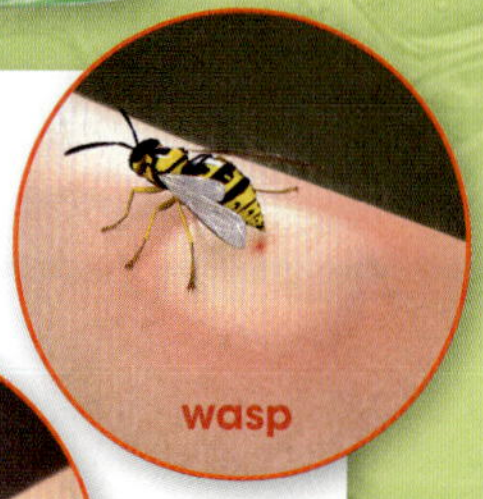
wasp

bee

Useful language

particle (n) *line 8*
reaction (n) *line 10*
dissolve (v) *line 13*
germ (n) *line 19*
paste (n) *line 35*

1 **Read the text quickly. Then answer the question.**

1 Which household cleaning products are mentioned in the text?

2 **Read the text again. Match the headings with the paragraphs.**

~~A~~ Chemicals in everyday life
B Dangerous chemicals
C Different kinds of acids
D How do chemicals clean things?
E Protecting the environment

3 **Answer the questions.**

What is an alkali?
An alkali is a chemical. It reacts in water and cleans things.

1 What is a mixture of an alkali and water called?

____

2 What kind of acid is there in fruit?

____

3 Why do you have to wear gloves if you use an acid?

____

4 What is a natural cleaning product?

____

5 What can you use if a wasp stings you?

____

4 **Complete the sentences with information from the text.**

Soap, dishwasher tablets, and washing powder are alkalis.

1 An alkali reacts with water and _______________

____

2 The new liquid _______________

____

3 Toilet cleaners must _______________

____

4 When you use an acid, you _______________

____

5 You can mix water with bicarbonate of soda _______________

____

Project

Think about household cleaning products you use. Find out what is in them and write a science report. Think about the following:

- What do you use them for?
- Are they acids or alkalis?
- How do they work?

THE SKY AT NIGHT

THE NORTHERN HEMISPHERE

THE SOUTHERN HEMISPHERE

If you look at the sky on a clear night, you'll be able to see about 2,000 stars. If you want to see more stars, you'll have to use a telescope. The stars you see are actually suns and they look so small because they are so far away. The Earth and the Sun are part of an enormous family group that contains millions of stars. This family group is called a galaxy. There are billions of galaxies in the Universe and our galaxy is called the Milky Way. The Milky Way is bigger than other galaxies in the Universe and astronomers think that there are about 100,000 million stars in the Milky Way.

Each galaxy has different constellations. A constellation is a pattern of stars. There are 88 constellations in the sky and astronomers use star maps to find them. If you live in the northern hemisphere, you will see different constellations from people in the southern hemisphere.

In each constellation, there are stars of different ages, sizes, color, and temperature. New stars are very bright and hot, 36,000°F and they look blue or sometimes white. Older stars are cooler, 7,500°F and they don't shine as brightly. They look orange or red. The biggest stars are red, but they are the coolest temperature, 5,500°F. The biggest stars in the galaxy are called supergiant stars, but they only live for a few million years. Smaller stars are called dwarf stars and they live longer than supergiant stars. When supergiant stars die, they explode. The explosion is called a supernova.

Different cultures see different patterns in the stars like kings, birds, bears, horses and the signs of the zodiac. One big constellation is called the Great Bear and seven stars in this form the Big Dipper. In ancient Mayan culture, they saw the Big Dipper as a parrot. The ancient Chinese saw a special chariot for a king.

So next time you look at the stars try and find a pattern: is it an animal, is it a bird, or could it be your star sign?

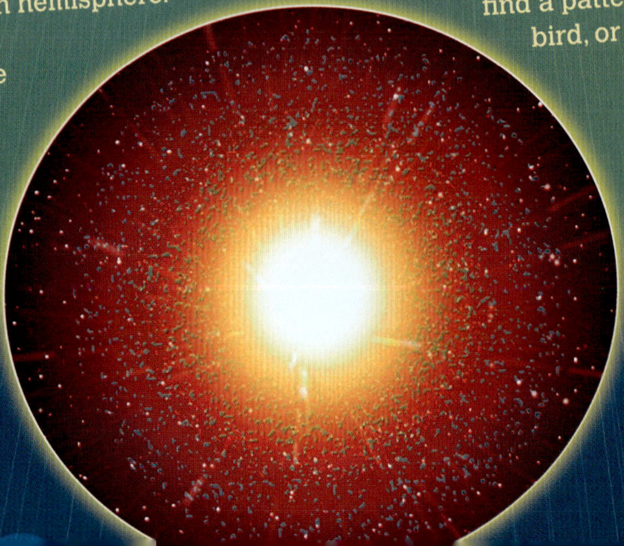

Useful language

pattern (n) *line 14*
hemisphere (n) *line 17*
explode (v) *line 33*
explosion (n) *line 33*
chariot (n) *line 39*

1 Read the text quickly. Then answer the question.

1 Which galaxy do we live in?

2 Read the text again. Match the questions and answers.

1 How many stars will you see on a clear night?
2 How many stars are there in the Milky Way?
3 How many constellations are there in the sky?
4 How hot are new stars?
5 How long do the biggest stars live for?
6 How many stars are there in the Big Dipper?

a 7
b 88
c 2000
d 36,000°F
e A few million years
f 100,000 million

3 Complete the table with information about the stars.

Star	Temperature	Color
new	36,000°F	1 ________
old	2 ________	3 ________
supergiant	4 ________	5 ________

4 Answer the questions.

What are stars?
Stars are suns.

1 What are galaxies?
____

2 What color are the hottest stars?
____

3 What is the name of the biggest stars in a galaxy?
____

4 What is a supernova?
____

5 What constellation does the Big Dipper belong to?
____

6 What did the ancient Mayans see in the Big Dipper?
____

Project

Write about your star sign constellation. Think about the following:

- What is your star sign?
- What does your star sign constellation look like?
- What other stars are near your stars?

THE GREEK MYTHS

Before people could write they told or sang stories and poems. Later, these stories became written poems or stories. Myths are stories and people often believe they are true, but usually the events aren't real. They are symbolic and they are a way of trying to explain the world. Myths began a long time ago and different cultures and countries have different myths. Some of the most famous myths have come from Greece.

Homer, a famous Greek writer, wrote two poems called *The Iliad* and *The Odyssey*. The poems are based on Greek myth. They are two of the oldest pieces of western literature and they have existed since the 8th century B.C.

The Iliad describes a short period of time in the last year of the Trojan War. King Agamemnon is the King of the Greeks. He is fighting a war with the Trojans. It has been a difficult war and it has continued for ten years. The story tells us how Odysseus, a Greek soldier, has tricked the Trojans. He has brought a huge wooden horse to the city of Troy and has left it in front of the city gates. The Trojans think that the horse is a present and take it into the city. Greek soldiers have hidden inside the horse and at night, the soldiers get out of the horse and open the city gates. The rest of the Greek army then enters the city of Troy and destroys it. The Greeks win the battle and Odysseus must now return home to the city of Ithaca.

After *The Iliad*, Homer wrote a sequel called *The Odyssey*. This poem begins at the end of the Trojan War and describes how Odysseus, the Greek hero, travels home. The Trojan War lasted ten years, but Odysseus has to travel for another ten years to reach home. On his way home, he faces many dangers. He meets a monster called a Cyclops and he has to travel through a dangerous storm. Odysseus has been away for almost twenty years and his wife and family think he is dead, but Odysseus survives the different dangers on his journey home. When he finally arrives in Ithaca he is reunited with his family and he becomes a great hero.

Useful language

fight (v) *line 25*
war (n) *line 25*
trick (v) *line 29*
sequel (n) *line 39*
journey (n) *line 50*

1 **Read the text quickly. Then answer the question.**

1 Who wrote *The Iliad* and *The Odyssey*?

2 **Read the text again. Are the sentences true or false?**

Myths are true stories. False

1 King Agamemnon is from Troy. ________

2 Homer wrote *The Odyssey* before *The Iliad*. ________

3 Odysseus is a Trojan soldier. ________

4 The horse the Greeks hide in is made of wood. ________

5 Odysseus has been away from his home for twenty years. ________

3 **Put the pictures from *The Iliad* in the correct order. Then write sentences using the simple present.**

a

b

c

d

e

f

1 Greek soldiers / hide / horse
The Greek soldiers hide inside the wooden horse.

2 Greek soldiers / leave / horse / city gates
____

3 Trojans / take / horse / city
____

4 Greek soldiers / get out of / horse
____

5 Greek soldiers / destroy / Troy
____

6 Odysseus and his men / return / Ithaca
____

Project

Find out about a myth in your country. Think about the following:

- Who are the main characters?
- Where does it take place?
- What happens?

Math around us

Math theories are everywhere and mathematicians are always trying to solve problems. Pythagoras was a Greek mathematician who lived more than 2000 years ago. Math students today still use his theorem in geometry. His theorem proves that in a right-angled triangle, the sum of the squares of the shorter sides equals the square of the longest side, or the hypotenuse. The equation to work this out is simple: $a^2 + b^2 = c^2$.

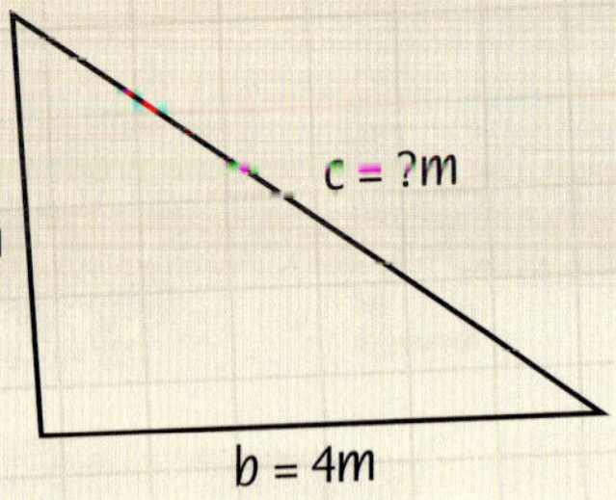

So, to calculate the length of c:

$3^2 + 4^2 = c^2$

$9 + 16 = c^2$

$25 = c^2$

$\sqrt{25} = 5$, so $c = 5m$

The Pythagorean theorem is used in many different ways in everyday life. For example, you can use the Pythagorean theorem in a baseball match. You can calculate how far the second baseman has to throw the ball to get the runner out before he reaches the home plate:

$27.36^2 + 27.36^2 = c^2$

$745.8336 + 745.8336 = c^2$

$1491.6672 = c^2$

$\sqrt{1491.6672} = 38.62$, so the second baseman has to throw the ball 38.62 m to reach the home plate.

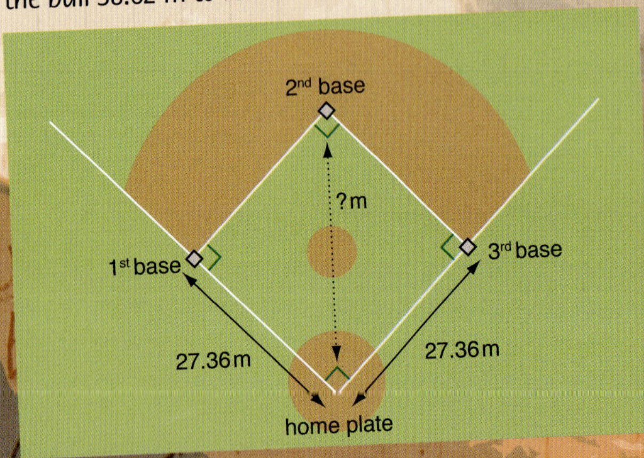

We also use algorithms every day in different areas of our lives. An algorithm is a list of instructions or rules that must be followed to solve a problem. An algorithm requires four things: data (what you want to do), a process (how you want to do it), a result, and any other information you need to do the task.

There are three different kinds of algorithms:

- ones we learn, for example arithmetic
- ones we work out for ourselves, for example finding a friend's phone number
- ones which require written instructions, for example reading directions or following a recipe.

We use arithmetic algorithms to solve a Sudoku puzzle. An example of an everyday algorithm which you work out for yourself is changing a light bulb. An algorithm for changing a light bulb could look like this:

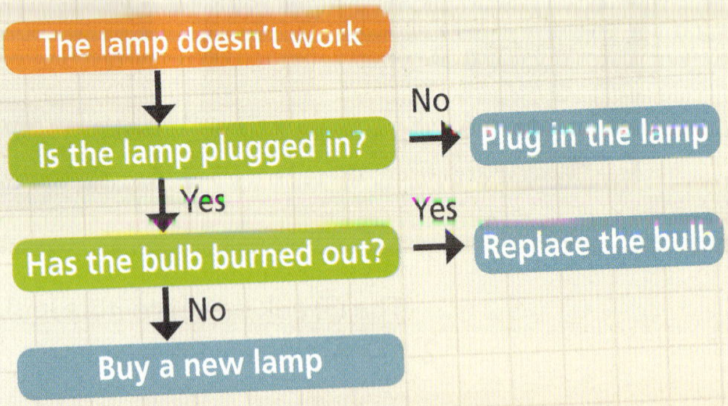

Written algorithms with special codes are used in computer programs. The codes are used because computers can't think and the instructions must be very clear.

Useful language

prove (v) *line 5*
sum (n) *line 6*
runner (n) *line 18*
home plate (n) *line 19*
light bulb (n) *line 40*
plug in (v) *line 42*
burn out (v) *line 43*

1 **Read the text quickly. Then answer the question.**

1 What two mathematical areas does the text mention?

2 **Read the text. Write *P* (Pythagoras) or *A* (Algorithm).**

He lived more than 2,000 years ago. P

1 One angle must measure 90°. ____
2 You can use it to solve a sudoku puzzle. ____
3 Computers use these with special codes. ____
4 You can use it in a baseball game. ____
5 You can use it when following a recipe. ____

3 **Read the text again. Answer the questions.**

What is the name of the longest side of a triangle?
It is called the hypotenuse.

1 What is the main idea in the Pythagorean theorem?
____
2 What is an algorithm?
____
3 How many things do you need to make an algorithm and what are they?
____
4 What are the three different types of algorithms?
____
5 Which type of algorithm do you use to solve a Sudoku?
____

4 **Work out these problems. Use the Pythagorean theorem.**

1 What is the width of the TV?

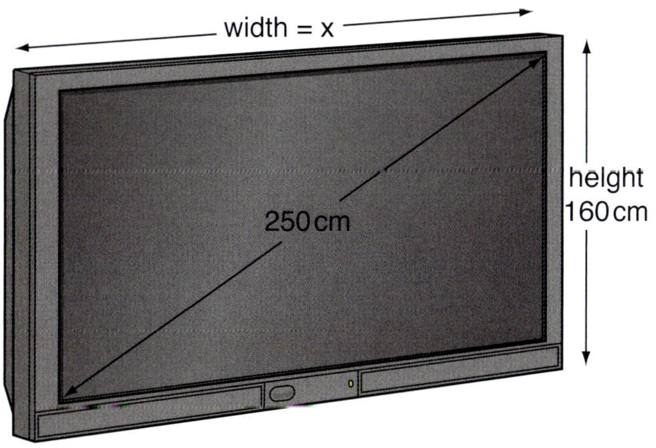

2 How long is the ladder?

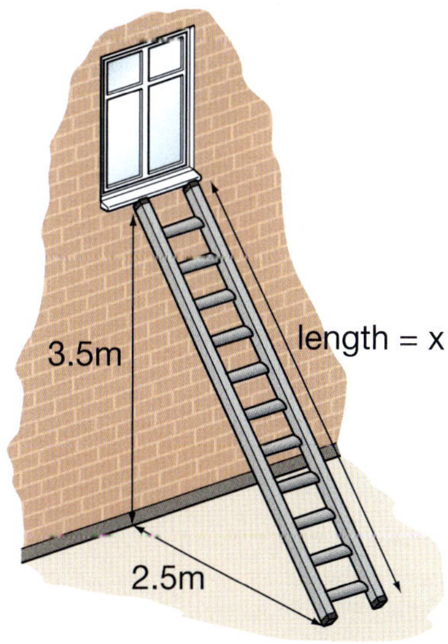

5 **Write an algorithm for sending a text message to a friend.**

6 **Write an algorithm for giving directions from your house to your school.**

Project

How do you use math in everyday life. Think about the following:

- When do you use geometry? Give an example.
- When do you use algorithms? Write an algorithm for something you do every day.

Word list

Unit 1

Places around town

bank /bæŋk/
bus station /ˈbʌs ˌsteɪʃn/
bus stop /ˈbʌs stɑp/
café /kæˈfeɪ/
church /tʃərtʃ/
hospital /ˈhɑspɪtl/
library /ˈlaɪbrɛri/
park /pɑrk/
parking lot /ˈpɑrkɪŋ ˌlɑt/
police station /pəˈlis ˌsteɪʃn/
post office /ˈpoʊst ˌɑfəs/
shopping mall /ʃɑpɪŋ mɔl/
sports center /ˌspɔrts ˈsɛntər/

Other nouns

adult /əˈdʌlt/
campground /ˈkæmpgraʊnd/
directions /dəˈrɛkʃn/
file /faɪl/
fire /ˈfaɪər/
ghost town /goʊst taʊn/
gold /goʊld/
gold rush /goʊld rʌʃ/
guideline /ˈgaɪdlaɪn/
hand signal /hænd ˈsɪgnəl/
helmet /ˈhɛlmət/
ingredient /ɪnˈgridiənt/
mine /maɪn/
mistake /mɪˈsteɪk/
official /əˈfɪʃl/
parking ticket /ˈpɑrkɪŋ ˌtɪkɪt/
password /ˈpæswərd/
pedestrian /pəˈdɛstriən/
picnic area /ˈpɪknɪk ˌɛriə/
pie /paɪ/
reception /rɪˈsɛpʃn/
roundabout /ˈraʊndəbaʊt/
rule /rul/
saloon /səˈlun/
silver /ˈsɪlvər/
ticket /ˈtɪkɪt/
traffic light /træfɪk laɪts/
truth /truθ/
turning /ˈtərnɪŋ/
virus /ˈvaɪrəs/
website /ˈwɛbsaɪt/

Verbs

contain /kənˈteɪn/
control /kənˈtroʊl/
copy /ˈkɑpi/
damage /ˈdæmɪdʒ/
discover /dɪsˈkʌvər/
download /ˈdaʊnloʊd/
enter /ˈɛntər/
share /ʃɛr/
store /stɔr/

Adjectives

absent /ˈæbsənt/
historic /hɪstɔrɪk/
luxury /ˈlʌkʃəri/
major /ˈmeɪdʒər/
online /ɑnˈlain/
personal /ˈpərsənl/
private /ˈpraɪvət/
public /ˈpʌblɪk/
secret /ˈsɪkrət/

Unit 2

Housework

clean my room /klin maɪ ˈrum/
clean the bathroom /klin θə ˈbæθrum/
do the cooking /du θə ˈkʊkɪŋ/
do the dusting /du θə ˈdʌstɪŋ/
do the ironing /du θə ˈaɪərnɪŋ/
do the grocery shopping /du θə ˈgroʊsəri ˌʃɑpɪŋ/
do the washing /du θə ˈwɑʃɪŋ/
lay / clear the table /leɪ, klɪr θə ˈteɪbl/
load / unload the dishwasher /loʊd, ˌʌnˈloʊd θə ˈdɪʃwɑʃər/
make my bed /ˌmeɪk maɪ ˈbɛd/
take out the trash /teɪk aʊt θə træʃ/
wash the dishes /wɑʃ θə dɪʃɪz/

Other nouns

advice /ədˈvaɪs/
after-school activity /ˈæftər skul ækˈtɪvəti/
allowance /əˈlaʊəns/
baby /ˈbeɪbi/
ballet /bæˈleɪ/
bathtub /ˈbæθtʌb/
beginner /bɪˈgɪnər/
chess /tʃɛs/
chore /tʃɔr/
corridor /ˈkɔrədɔr/
credit /ˈkrɛdət/
driver /ˈdraɪvər/
elimination /ɪˌlɪməˈneɪʃn/
episode /ˈɛpəsoʊd/
hit /hɪt/
host /hoʊst/
lady /ˈleɪdi/
mess /mɛs/
millionaire /ˌmɪlyəˈnɛr/
mission /ˈmɪʃn/
organization /ˌɔrgənəˈzeɪʃn/
repetition /ˌrɛpəˈtɪʃn/
sink /sɪŋk/
success /səkˈsɛs/
survey /ˈsərveɪ/
uniform /ˈyunəfɔrm/
volleyball training /ˈvɑlibəl ˌtreɪnɪŋ/

Verbs

save /seɪv/
spend /spɛnd/

Adjectives

average /ˈævrɪdʒ/
basic /ˈbeɪsɪk/
delicate /ˈdɛlɪkət/
dirty /ˈdərti/
extra /ˈɛkstrə/
foreign /ˈfɔrən/
part-time /ˈpɑrt ˌtaɪm/
professional /prəˈfɛʃənl/
recent /ˈrisənt/

Adverbs

generally /ˈdʒɛnərəli/
luckily /ˈlʌkəli/

Review A

Nouns

medical certificate /ˈmɛdɪkl sərˈtɪfəkət/
paper round /ˈpeɪpər raʊnd/
participant /pɑrˈtɪsəpənt/

Verbs

borrow /ˈbɑroʊ/
deliver /dɪˈlɪvər/

Culture club A

Nouns

area /ˈɛriə/
borough /ˈbəroʊ/
century /ˈsɛntʃəri/
coast /koʊst/
immigrant /ˈɪməgrənt/
liberty /ˈlɪbərti/
native /ˈneɪtɪv/
resident /ˈrɛzədənt/

Verbs

create /kriˈeɪt/
mix /mɪks/
settle /ˈsɛtl/

Unit 3

Personality

ambitious /æmˈbɪʃəs/
bossy /ˈbɔsi/
confident /ˈkɑnfədənt/
creative /kriˈeɪtɪv/
friendly /ˈfrɛndli/
hard-working /hɑrd ˈwərkɪŋ/
kind /kaɪnd/
lazy /ˈleɪzi/
organized /ˈɔrgənaɪzd/
outgoing /ˌaʊtˈgoʊɪŋ/
patient /ˈpeɪʃnt/
selfish /ˈsɛlfɪʃ/
serious /ˈsɪriəs/
shy /ʃaɪ/
stubborn /ˈstʌbərn/

Nouns

acrobat /ˈækrəbæt/
Aquarius /əˈkwɛriəs/
ambition /æmˈbɪʃn/
Aries /ˈɛriz/
astrology /əˈstrɑlədʒi/
Cancer /ˈkænsər/
Capricorn /ˈkæprɪkɔrn/
characteristic /ˌkærəktəˈrɪstɪk/
circus /ˈsərkəs/
degree /dɪˈgri/
department /dɪˈpɑrtmənt/
designer /dɪˈzaɪnər/
doctor /ˈdɑktər/
element /ˈɛləmənt/
events organizer /ɪˌvɛnts ˈɔrgənaɪzər/
exhibition /ˌɛksəˈbɪʃn/
experience /ɪkˈspɪriəns/
festival /ˈfɛstəvl/
games tester /geɪmz ˈtɛstər/
Gemini /ˈdʒɛmənaɪ/
gymnastics /dʒɪmˈnæstɪks/
horoscope /ˈhɔrəskoʊp/
Leo /ˈlioʊ/
Libra /ˈlibrə/
martial arts /ˈmɑrʃl ɑrts/
Pisces /ˈpaɪsiz/
planet /ˈplænət/
position /pəˈzɪʃn/
practice /ˈpræktəs/
Sagittarius /ˌsædʒəˈtɛriəs/
Scorpio /ˈskɔrpioʊ/
star sign /ˈstɑr saɪn/
Taurus /ˈtɔrəs/
Virgo /ˈvərgoʊ/
wheel /wil/
zodiac /ˈzoʊdiæk/

Verbs

depend /dɪˈpɛnd/
divide /dəˈvaɪd/
influence /ˈɪnfluəns/
prepare /prɪˈpɛr/

Other adjectives

ancient /ˈeɪnʃənt/
compatible /kəmˈpætəbl/
emotional /ɪˈmoʊʃənl/
final /ˈfaɪnl/
intellectual /ˌɪntəˈlɛktʃuəl/
intense /ɪnˈtɛns/
methodical /mɛˈθɑdɪkl/
nonsense /ˈnɑnsɛns/
sceptical /ˈskɛptɪkl/
stable /ˈsteɪbl/
unusual /ʌnˈyuʒuəl/

Adverbs

intuitive /ɪnˈtuətɪv/

Unit 4

The weather

cloudy /'klaʊdi/
cold /koʊld/
foggy /'fɔgi/
freezing /'frizɪŋ/
hot /hɑt/
mild /maɪld/
raining /'reɪnɪŋ/
snowing /'snoʊɪŋ/
sunny /'sʌni/
warm /wɔrm/
windy /'wɪndi/

Nouns

accident /'æksədənt/
air conditioning /ɛr kən'dɪʃnɪŋ/
aluminum /ə'lumənəm/
aspect /'æspɛkt/
caiman /'keɪmən/
carbon dioxide /ˌkɑrbən daɪ'ɑksaɪd/
carbon footprint /ˌkɑrbən 'fʊtprɪnt/
champion /'tʃæmpiən/
climate /'klaɪmət/
effect /ɪ'fɛkt/
electricity /ɪˌlɛk'trɪsəti/
environment /ɛn'vaɪərnmənt/
expedition /'ɛkspə'dɪʃn/
explorer /ɪk'splɔrər/
gas /gæs/
global warming /'gloʊbl wɔrmɪŋ/
greenhouse gases /'grinhaʊs ˌgæsɪs/
jaguar /'dʒægwɑr/
journey /'dʒərni/
key /ki/
lamp /læmp/
picnic /'pɪknɪk/
piranha fish /pə'rɑnə fɪʃ/
plastic bag /'plæstɪk bæg/
prediction /prɪ'dɪkʃn/
questionnaire /kwɛstʃə'nɛr/
rainforest /'reɪnˌfɔrəst/
rainwater /'reinˌwɔtər/
temperature /'tɛmprətʃər/
wild animal /waɪld 'ænəml/

Verbs

calculate /'kælkyəleɪt/
contribute /kən'trɪbyut/
measure /'mɛʒər/
panic /'pænɪk/
protect /prə'tɛkt/
succeed /sək'sid/
supply /sə'plaɪ/
surround /sə'raʊnd/

Other adjectives

everyday /'ɛvrideɪ/
extinct /ɪk'stɪŋkt/
heavy /'hɛvi/
in fashion /ɪn 'fæʃn/
rare /rɛr/
tropical /'trɑpɪkl/
weak /wik/

Adverbs

directly /də'rɛktli/

Review B

Nouns

charity /'tʃærəti/
weather forecast /'wɛðər 'fɔrkæst/

Verbs

celebrate /'sɛləbreɪt/

Culture club B

Nouns

atmosphere /'ætməsfɪr/
climatologist /ˌklaɪmə'tɑlədʒɪst/
crop /krɑp/
economist /ɪ'kɑnəmɪst/
expert /'ɛkspərt/
hail /heɪl/
incident /'ɪnsədənt/
lemon /'lɛmən/
meteorologist /ˌmitiə'rɑlədʒɪst/
phenomenon /fə'nɑmənən/
ski resort /ski rɪ'zɔrt/

Verbs

destroy /dɪ'strɔɪ/
postpone /poʊst'poʊn/
sculpt /skʌlpt/

Unit 5

Exciting experiences

do a parachute jump /du ə 'pærəʃut dʒʌmp/
fly in an airplane /flaɪ ɪn ən 'ɛrpleɪn/
go camping /goʊ 'kæmpɪŋ/
go scuba diving /goʊ 'skubə ˌdaɪvɪŋ/
meet a famous person /mit ə 'feɪməs ˌpərsn/
ride a roller coaster /raɪd ə 'roʊlə rkoʊstər/
stay in a hotel /ˌsteɪ ɪn ə hoʊ'tɛl/
travel abroad /ˌtrævl ə'brɔd/
watch a soccer game /wɑtʃ ə 'sɑkər geɪm/

Nouns

bowling lane /'boʊlɪŋ ˌleɪn/
bungee jump /'bʌndʒi dʒʌmp/
camel /'kæml/
contact /'kɑntækt/
dance course /dæns kɔrs/
food poisoning /'fud ˌpɔɪznɪŋ/
hill /hɪl/
marathon /'mærəθɑn/
reef /rif/
sabbatical /sə'bætɪkl/
swimming costume /'swɪmɪŋ ˌkɑstum/
tower /'taʊər/
washing machine /'wɑʃɪŋ məˌʃin/

Other verbs

book /bʊk/
canoe /kə'nu/
hydro-zorbing /'haɪdroʊ zɔrbɪŋ/
invent /ɪn'vɛnt/
ride a horse /raɪd ə hɔrs/
roll /roʊl/

Adjectives

honest /'ɑnəst/
normal /'nɔrml/

Adverbs

completely /kəm'plitli/

Unit 6

Books

autobiography /ˌɔtəbaɪ'ɑgrəfi/
biography /baɪ'ɑgrəfi/
detective / crime story /dɪ'tɛktɪv, kraɪm ˌstɔri/
fantasy story /'fæntəsi ˌstɔri/
horror story /'hɔrər ˌstɔri/
love story /'lʌv ˌstɔri/
science fiction story /saɪəns 'fɪkʃn ˌstɔri/
spy story /'spaɪ ˌstɔri/

Other nouns

agent /'eɪdʒənt/
alien universe /'eɪliən ˌyunəvərs/
bestseller /ˌbɛst'sɛlər/

boss /bɔs/
discount /'dɪskaʊnt/
expression /ɪk'sprɛʃn/
gun /gʌn/
motive /'moʊtɪv/
princess /'prɪnsəs/
prize /praɪz/
receipt /rɪ'sit/
sale /seɪl/
secret service /'sikrət ˌsərvəs/
shock /ʃɑk/
souvenir /ˌsuvə'nɪr/
special forces /'spɛʃl ˌfɔrsɪz/

Verbs

admit /əd'mɪt/
increase /'ɪnkris/
insist /ɪn'sɪst/
kill /kɪl/
murder /'mərdər/
pour /pɔr/
record /rɪ'kɔrd/
risk /rɪsk/

Adjectives

classic /'klæsɪk/
empty /'ɛmpti/
mysterious /mɪ'stɪriəs/
successful /sək'sɛsfl/
top secret /tɑp 'sikrət/

Adverbs

exactly /ɪg'zæktli/

Review C

Nouns

apartment /ə'pɑrtmənt/
downtown /ˌdaʊn'taʊn/
extraterrestrial /ˌɛkstrətə'rɛstriəl/
term /tərm/

Culture club C

Nouns

bald eagle /bɔld 'igl/
bear /bɛr/
boat trip /'boʊt trɪp/
cultural group /'kʌltʃərəl grup/
floatplane /'floʊtpleɪn/
fortune /'fɔrtʃən/
frontier /frʌn'tɪr/
glacier /'gleɪʃər/
hump /hʌmp/
orca /'ɔrkə/
sea lion /'si ˌlaɪən/
valley /'væli/
waterfall /'wɔtərfɔl/
whale /weɪl/
wildlife /'waɪldlaɪf/

Verbs

hunt /hʌnt/
relive /ˌri'lɪv/

Adjectives

spectacular /spɛk'tækyələr/
traditional /trə'dɪʃnl/

Unit 7

Crime

kidnap someone /'kɪdnæp ˌsʌmwʌn/
kidnapper /'kɪdnæpər/
mug someone /'mʌg ˌsʌmwʌn/
mugger /'mʌgər/
murder someone /'mərdər ˌsʌmwʌn/
murderer /'mərdərər/
pick someone's pocket /ˌpɪk sʌmwʌns 'pɑkət/
pickpocket /'pɪkpɑkət/
rob a bank /rɑb ə 'bæŋk/
robber /'rɑbər/

Word list

shoplift /ˈʃɑplɪft/
shoplifter /ˈʃɑplɪftər/
steal a painting /stil ə ˈpeɪntɪŋ/
thief /θif/
vandal /ˈvændl/
vandalize a building /ˈvændlaɪz ə ˈbɪldɪŋ/

Other nouns

case /keɪs/
curse /kərs/
death /dɛθ/
phone box /foʊn bɑks/
suspect /ˈsʌspɛkt/
victim /ˈvɪktəm/
wallet /ˈwɑlət/

Verbs

die /daɪ/
follow /ˈfɑloʊ/
hit /hɪt/
lock /lɑk/
run away /rʌn əˈweɪ/
report /rɪˈpɔrt/
smoke a pipe /smoʊk ə paɪp/
cross the road /krɔs θə roʊd/

Adjectives

alone /əˈloʊn/
monstrous /ˈmɑnstrəs/

Unit 8

Human achievement

architect /ˈɑrkətɛkt/
artist /ˈɑrtɪst/
composer /kəmˈpoʊzər/
explorer /ɪkˈsplɔrər/
inventor /ɪnˈvɛntər/
politician /ˌpɑləˈtɪʃn/
scientist /ˈsaɪəntɪst/
writer /ˈraɪtər/

Other nouns

aqua globe /ˈækwə gloʊb/
bacteria /bækˈtɪriə/
basis /ˈbeɪsəs/
component /kəmˈpoʊnənt/
gadget /ˈgædʒət/
gas lamp /gæs ˈlæmp/
genetic code /dʒəˈnɛtɪk koʊd/
genius /ˈdʒinyəs/
hard drive /ˈhɑrd draɪv/
hypertext /ˈhaɪpərtɛkst/
laboratory /ˈlæbrətɔri/
law of gravity /lɔ əv ˈgrævəti/
microchip /ˈmaɪkroʊtʃɪp/
miniskirt /ˈmɪniskərt/
molecule /ˈmɑləkyul/
network /ˈnɛtwərk/
penicillin /ˌpɛnəˈsɪlən/
plate /pleɪt/
program /ˈproʊgræm/
ring /rɪŋ/
signal /ˈsɪgnəl/
speaker /ˈspikər/
substance /ˈsʌbstəns/
web browser /ˈwɛb ˌbraʊzər/

Verbs

access /ˈæksɛs/
attach /əˈtætʃ/
back up /ˈbæk ʌp/
compose /kəmˈpoʊz/
connect /kəˈnɛkt/
consider /kənˈsɪdər/
cut /kʌt/
debate /dɪˈbeɪt/
demonstrate /ˈdɛmənstreɪt/
develop /dɪˈvɛləp/
nominate /ˈnɑməneɪt/
receive /rɪˈsiv/
send /sɛnd/
transmit /trænsˈmɪt/
work out /wərk aʊt/

Adjectives

electronic /ɪˌlɛkˈtrɑnɪk/
external /ɪkˈstərnl/
impossible /ɪmˈpɑsəbl/
influential /ˌɪnfluˈɛnʃl/
radioactive /ˌreɪdioʊˈæktɪv/
similar /ˈsɪmələr/
transatlantic /ˌtrænzətˈlæntɪk/
waterproof /ˈwɔtərpruf/

Review D

Nouns

bench /bɛntʃ/
inquiry /ˈɪnkwəri/
purse /pərs/
security camera /səˈkyʊrəti ˌkæmrə/
sushi bar /ˈsuʃi bɑr/

Verbs

crash /kræʃ/
escape /ɪˈskeɪp/

Culture club D

Nouns

discipline /ˈdɪsəplɪn/
grades /greɪdz/
hero /ˈhiroʊ/
program /ˈproʊgræm/
rate /reɪt/
recipe /ˈrɛsəpi/

Verbs

honor /ˈɑnər/
negotiate /nəˈgoʊʃieɪt/
survive /sərˈvaɪv/
vote /voʊt/

Adjectives

spectacular /spɛkˈtækyələr/
traditional /trəˈdɪʃnl/

Curriculum extra A

Nouns

acid /ˈæsɪd/
alkali /ˈælkəlaɪ/
bee /bi/
chemical /ˈkɛmɪkl/
citric acid /ˈsɪtrɪk ˌæsɪd/
dishwasher tablet /ˈdɪʃwaʃər ˌtæblət/
emulsion /ɪˈmʌlʃn/
hydrogen /ˈhaɪdrədʒən/
metal /ˈmɛtl/
oven /ˈʌvən/
particle /ˈpɑrtɪkl/
paste /peɪst/
skin /skɪn//
vinegar /ˈvɪnɪgər/
wasp /wɑsp/

Verbs

attract /əˈtrækt/
burn /bərn
combine /kəmˈbaɪn/
dissolve /dɪˈzɑlv/
react /riˈækt/
sting /stɪŋ/
touch /tʌtʃ/

Adjectives

plant-based /plænt beɪsd/

Curriculum extra B

Nouns

astronomer /əˈstrɑnəmər/
billion /ˈbɪlyən/
chariot /ˈtʃæriət/
constellation /ˌkɑnstəˈleɪʃn/
explosion /ɪkˈsploʊʒn/
galaxy /ˈgæləksi/
hemisphere /ˈhɛməsfɪr/
parrot /ˈpærət/
pattern /ˈpætərn/
sky /skaɪ/
supernova /ˌsupərˈnoʊvə/
telescope /ˌtɛləskoʊp/

Adjectives

clear /klɪr/
dwarf /dwɔrf/

Curriculum extra C

Nouns

army /ˈɑrmi/
battle /ˈbætl/
city gate /ˈsɪti geɪt/
myth /mɪθ/
sequel /ˈsɪkwəl/
war /wɔr/

Verbs

exist /ɪgˈzɪst/
fight /faɪt/
trick /trɪk/

Adjectives

reunited /ˌriyuˈnaɪtɪd/
symbolic /sɪmˈbɑlɪk/

Curriculum extra D

Nouns

algorithm /ˈælgərɪðəm/
angle /ˈæŋgl/
arithmetic /əˈrɪθmətɪk/
base /beɪs/
baseman /ˌbeɪsmən/
code /koʊd/
diamond /ˈdaɪmənd/
equation /ɪˈkweɪʒn/
geometry /dʒiˈɑmətri/
home plate /hoʊm pleɪt/
hypotenuse /haɪˈpɑtənuz/
light bulb /laɪt bʌlb/
mathematician /ˌmæθməˈtɪʃn/
puzzle /ˈpʌzl/
recipe /ˈrɛsəpi/
right angle /raɪt ˈæŋgl/
sum /sʌm/
task /tæsk/
theory /ˈθɪri/

Verbs

burn out /bərn aʊt/
plug in /plʌg ɪn/
prove /pruv/
replace /rɪˈpleɪs/

Got it!

Level 2

Workbook

Philippa Bowen & Denis Delaney

1 Grammar rules

must
Affirmative and negative

Affirmative	
I **must** go	it **must** go
you **must** go	we **must** go
he **must** go	you **must** go
she **must** go	they **must** go

Subject + | ***must*** | **+ base form of the verb**

Negative	
Full form	**Short form**
I **must not** go	I **mustn't** go
you **must not** go	you **mustn't** go
he **must not** go	he **mustn't** go
she **must not** go	she **mustn't** go
it **must not** go	it **mustn't** go
we **must not** go	we **mustn't** go
you **must not** go	you **mustn't** go
they **must not** go	they **mustn't** go

Subject + | ***must not (mustn't)*** | **+ base form of the verb**

1 ***Must* is a modal verb. All modal verbs follow the same rules:**
- **We only use one form for all persons.**
I **must** study. He **must** study.
We **must** study. They **must** study.
- **We do not add an *-s* to *must* with he, she, or it.**
He **must** study. NOT ~~He musts study~~.
- **We always follow *must* with another verb in the base form.**
You **must eat** this pizza.
NOT ~~You must to eat this pizza~~.
You **mustn't go** to school.
NOT ~~You mustn't to go to school~~.
- **We don't use *don't / doesn't* with the negative form of modal verbs.**
You **mustn't** talk.
NOT ~~You don't must talk~~.

2 **The negative form of *must* is *must not*. In spoken and informal written English, *must not* is usually abbreviated to *mustn't*.**
You must not shout. = You **mustn't** shout.

3 **We use *must* to talk about necessity. Necessity means that you cannot avoid doing something.**
You **must** come home before 9:30 p.m. (*You cannot come home after 9:30 p.m.*)
I **must** call Mel. It's her birthday today. (*You cannot call Mel tomorrow because it is her birthday today.*)
I **must** do my homework now. (*You cannot do your homework later because you are busy.*)

4 **We use *must* to express general obligation.**
You **must** drive on the right in the U.S.

5 **We use *mustn't* to express prohibition.**
You **mustn't** use a dictionary in the test!
You **mustn't** use your cell phone in class.

Compounds: *some / any / no*

	Person	Thing	Place
some	some**one** / some**body**	some**thing**	some**where**
any	any**one** / any**body**	any**thing**	any**where**
no	no **one** / no**body**	no**thing**	no**where**

1 **We use *-one / -body* to talk about people.**

2 **We use *-thing* to talk about things and objects.**

3 **We use *-where* to talk about places.**

4 **We use the compound *some* in affirmative sentences.**
Someone / **Somebody** is at the door.
There's always **something** interesting to do.
I want to go **somewhere** today.

5 **We use the compound *any* in negative and interrogative sentences.**
There isn't **anyone** / **anybody** at the door.
Is there **anyone** / **anybody** at the door?
There isn't **anything** interesting to do.
Is there **anything** interesting to do?
I don't want to go **anywhere** today.
Do you want to go **anywhere** interesting today?

6 **We use *no* in affirmative sentences to mean something does not exist.**
There's **no one** / **nobody** in the classroom.
The teacher said **nothing** about doing extra homework.
There's **nowhere** to go swimming in Highmore.

Watch out!

In English, only one negative is used. In a sentence with *no*, we use the verb in the affirmative form.

There's **nothing** on TV.

NOT ~~There isn't nothing on TV~~.

I know **no one** in my new school.

NOT ~~I don't know no one in my new school~~.

Compounds: *every*

	Person	Thing	Place
every	every**one** / every**body**	every**thing**	every**where**

1 **We use the compound *every* to talk about all people, objects, or places.**
Everyone / **Everybody** is here.
Everything is ready.
We went **everywhere** in the museum.

2 **We use the compound *every* in affirmative, negative, and interrogative forms.**
Everyone / **Everybody** came to my party.
We didn't have **everything** ready.
Did you go **everywhere** in the museum?

3 **We use the compound *everyone* / *everybody* with a singular verb.**
Everyone likes Lady Gaga.
Everybody in my class is from Brazil.

Word list

Places around town
bank ______
bus station ______
bus stop ______
café ______
church ______
hospital ______
library ______
park ______
parking lot ______
police station ______
post office ______
shopping mall ______
sports center ______

Student Book pp. 12–13, p.15

1 Exercises

Vocabulary

Places around town

1 Match the word halves.

1	shopping	a	office
2	police	b	stop
3	sports	c	mall
4	parking	d	center
5	post	e	station
6	bus	f	lot

2 Read the descriptions. Then write the place name.

There are a lot of different stores here.
shopping mall

1 People go to this place when they aren't well or when they have an accident.
h ________________

2 You can usually swim and play other sports here.
s ________________ ________________

3 There are a lot of books here. People can borrow them and take them home for two or three weeks.
l ________________

4 You usually come here when you lose your passport or cell phone.
p ________________ ________________

5 Some people go to this place on Sundays. They sing and pray here.
c ________________

6 You can send mail and parcels here.
p ________________ ________________

7 There are trees and flowers here. You can walk and relax, and sometimes there's a play area for children.
p ________________

8 People come here to change money.
b ________________

9 You usually pay to leave your car here.
p ________________ ________________

10 People come here to have a drink. They sometimes eat here, too.
c ________________

Grammar

must / mustn't

3 Complete the sentences with *must* (✓) or *mustn't* (✗) and the verbs in the box.

clean do eat go
~~send~~ study watch

You mustn't send text messages in class! (✓)

1 I ________________ for the math exam. (✓)

2 You ________________ food in your bedroom. (✗)

3 I ________________ my homework in front of the TV. (✗)

4 The boys ________________ straight home after school. (✓)

5 Katia ________________ TV after 10 p.m. (✗)

6 Girls! You ________________ your room. It's awful. (✓)

4 Read the information about Ocean County Library. Then complete the rules with *must* or *mustn't* and a verb.

OCEAN COUNTY LIBRARY
Information for library members

- You can borrow a maximum of four books, but please return them to the library after two weeks.
- You can only read dictionaries in the library. Don't take them home.
- Please don't use cell phones or talk loudly in the library.
- Please don't eat or drink in the library.
- You can use the computers, but please get a password from the information desk.

LIBRARY RULES

- **You mustn't borrow more than four books.**
- **You [1] ________________ your books to the library after two weeks.**
- **You [2] ________________ the dictionaries home.**
- **You [3] ________________ cell phones or talk loudly.**
- **You [4] ________________ or drink.**
- **You [5] ________________ your password from the information desk.**

Compounds: *some / any / no*

5 Complete the sentences with *some*, *any*, or *no* using *-thing*, *-where*, or *-body*.

We're not going anywhere this weekend.
Nobody came to soccer practice today!

1 I'm bored! I don't have ______________ to do!
2 The cat isn't ______________ in the yard.
3 This math problem is really difficult. Does ______________ know the answer?
4 They live ______________ in Delaware.
5 There is ______________ good on TV tonight. Let's watch a DVD.
6 There is ______________ to go. It's boring here.
7 I didn't see ______________ from my grade at the party.
8 Jack wants ______________ to eat.

6 Write sentences in affirmative (+), negative (-), or interrogative (?) forms.

There's someone in the classroom. (?)
Is there anyone in the classroom?

1 I didn't do anything interesting on the weekend. (+)
____
2 Did Helen go anywhere on Sunday? (-)
____
3 There was someone at the bus stop. (?)
____
4 You have something in your bag. (?)
____
5 I know somebody in that school. (-)
____
6 Kevin didn't say anything. (+)
____

Compounds: *every*

7 Write five sentences using the phrases in A, B, and C.

A	B	C
Are you inviting	everything	in our car.
Mom does	everyone	on their vacation.
We went	everywhere	in my school.
Does Kelly have		to your party?
They cycled		in our house.
I don't know		for her trip?

Are you inviting everyone to your party?

1 ______________
2 ______________
3 ______________
4 ______________
5 ______________

Round-up

8 Read Mia's e-mail. Choose the correct answers.

Hi, Zoe
Hello from Woodsboro – my new town. It's very small and it's *very* boring! There's a post office, a store, and a church, but **anything / nothing** exciting happens here!
Everyone in the town [1]**is / are** friendly, but there's [2]**no one / anyone** my age and there's [3]**anything / nothing** to do! I go to school in Union Bridge, a town near Woodsboro. I only started two days ago and, at the moment [4]**nothing / everything** at school is new! We [5]**must / mustn't** change classroom after every lesson, but I don't know where the classrooms are! There are a lot of rules at my new school. We [6]**must / mustn't** use our cell phones and we [7]**must / mustn't** talk during lessons. We [8]**must / mustn't** run in the corridors and we mustn't eat [9]**something / anything** in the classrooms! It's difficult to remember [10]**something / everything**!
Anyway, I must stop now because I have some homework for tomorrow.
Love,
Mia.

9 Correct the mistakes in the sentences below.

Mia lives in Union Bridge.
Mia lives in Woodsboro.

1 A lot of exciting things happen in the town.
____
2 Nobody is friendly in Woodsboro.
____
3 There are some people of Mia's age in Woodsboro.
____
4 There are a lot of things to do.
____
5 Mia's new school doesn't have any rules.
____
6 The students mustn't leave their classrooms after a lesson at school.
____
7 They must run in the corridors and they must eat their lunch in the classrooms.
____

Asking for and giving directions

1 Complete the dialogue with the phrases in the box.

as far as the | at the traffic lights | go up | ~~how do I get to~~ | opposite

A Excuse me. How do I get to the bank, please?

B Go down Springwood Avenue [1]__________ roundabout. Turn left and [2]__________ East Street. Go straight on [3]__________ and the bank is on the left. It's [4]__________ the church.

A Thanks.

2 Where do the people want to go? Look at the map. Then read the directions and complete the questions with the name of the place.

You are at the shopping mall.

A Excuse me. How do I get to the bank please?

B Go out of the shopping mall and cross the road. Go down Black Tail Boulevard as far as the traffic lights then turn left. It's on the left, next to the post office.

1 You are at the market.

A Excuse me. Can you tell me the way to the __________, please?

B Yes, sure. Go out of the market and go to the end of this road. Turn right at the junction and go down Poindexter Street as far as the traffic lights. Turn left. It's on the right, opposite a church.

2 You are at the parking lot.

A Excuse me. How do I get to the __________, please?

B Go out of the parking lot and turn right. Cross Hemon Street and go down Utah Street. At the end of the road, opposite the sports center, turn left. Take the first left and it's at the end of the road.

3 You are at the library.

A Excuse me. Can you tell me how to get to the __________, please?

B Yes, of course. Go out of the library and turn right. Take the first turning on the right and walk down the road to Poindexter Street. Turn left onto Poindexter Street and then take the second left. It's on the left, near the church.

4 You are at the bank.

A Excuse me. Can you tell me the way to the __________, please?

B Yes, sure. Turn right outside the bank and walk to Black Tail Boulevard. Turn right at the traffic lights and walk to the shopping mall. At the shopping mall, turn right and walk to the end of the road. It's on the right.

Student Book p.14

Reading

1 Read the text. Then match the sentence halves.

1 Arthur a is a religious community in the U.S.
2 Amish b is a list of rules.
3 Ordnung c is a town in Illinois.

A quiet life

Arthur is a small town in the U.S. It's in the state of Illinois, 250 km south of Chicago. In some ways it is a typical town. It has a small town center with some stores, a bank, a post office, and a few restaurants, but there's also something very different about Arthur. Some of the houses are modern but some houses don't have electricity or phones. Then, in the parking lots you can see horses and carts next to the cars. That is because a lot of Amish people live there.

The Amish are an old religious community. They originally came from Switzerland and Germany in the 18th century. They left Europe to escape religious persecution and a lot of them went to live in America. Today the Amish live in small communities in the states of Ohio, Pennsylvania, Iowa, and Illinois. They live very simple lives.

The Amish community has a lot of rules, or Ordnung. These rules tell them what they must and mustn't do. For example, they mustn't drive cars, use phones, or have electricity in their homes. There are also rules about their clothes and hair. Amish women and girls must wear long dresses and the men must wear dark jackets and pants. Women mustn't cut their hair short and men must have beards. Some of the rules are strict, but the Amish are happy to follow them because they like their traditional way of life.

2 Read the text again. Then answer the questions.

1 Why is Arthur different to other small towns in the U.S?
2 Where did the Amish originally come from?
3 When and why did they leave Europe?
4 What do Amish rules say about transportation and technology?
5 What rules are there about clothes and hair?

Writing

3 Read what Rebecca, an Amish student, says about her school. Then write a paragraph comparing it to your school. Write about:

- the age of students (from … to …)
- the number of students in a class
- the number of classrooms in your school
- the subjects you must study at school
- the length of your school day

"Amish children must start school when they are six years old and they finish at fourteen. We usually go to school from 9 a.m. to 3 p.m. There are nineteen children in my school and we all have lessons in one classroom. At school we must study math, English, German, geography, history and music." Rebecca

Student Book pp.16–17

2 Grammar rules

have to
Affirmative and negative

Affirmative	
I **have to** go	it **has to** go
you **have to** go	we **have to** go
he **has to** go	you **have to** go
she **has to** go	they **have to** go

Subject +	*have / has to*	+ base form of the verb

1 We use *have to* to express an external necessity or obligation.
I **have to** call my grandpa. It's his birthday.
Miku **has to** go the doctor's.

2 We use *have to* to express a necessity in the present or in the future.
I **have to** send this e-mail now.
Edu **has to** get up early tomorrow morning for school.

Negative
I **don't have to** go
you **don't have to** go
he **doesn't have to** go
she **doesn't have to** go
it **doesn't have to** go
we **don't have to go**
you **don't have to** go
they **don't have to** go

Subject +	*don't have to / doesn't have to*	+ base form of the verb

- **We use the negative forms *don't have to* / *doesn't have to* when there is no necessity or obligation.**
  In the U.S., students **don't have to** wear school uniform.
  She **doesn't have to** pay for the tickets now.

have to
Interrogative and short answers

Interrogative	
Do I **have to** go?	**Does** it **have to** go?
Do you **have to** go?	**Do** we **have to** go?
Does he **have to** go?	**Do** you **have to** go?
Does she **have to** go?	**Do** they **have to** go?

Do / Does	+ subject +	*have to*	+ base form of the verb

Short answers	
Affirmative	Negative
Yes, I **do**.	No, I **don't**.
Yes, you **do**.	No, you **don't**.
Yes, he **does**.	No, he **doesn't**.
Yes, she **does**.	No, she **doesn't**.
Yes, it **does**.	No, it **doesn't**.
Yes, you **do**.	No, you **don't**.
Yes, we **do**.	No, we **don't**.
Yes, they **do**.	No, they **don't**.

Yes,	+ subject pronoun +	*do / does*.
No,	+ subject pronoun +	*don't / doesn't*.

- **We use the auxiliary verb *do* with *have to* in the interrogative and short answer forms.**
  Do I have to get up early tomorrow?
  NOT ~~Have I to get up early tomorrow?~~
  Yes, you **do**. / No, you **don't**.
  NOT ~~Yes, you have~~. / ~~No, you don't have~~.

have to / must

- ***Have to* and *must* have a similar meaning. Both forms show a necessity or an obligation, but their uses are different.**
  - **We use *have to* to show an obligation which the speaker sees as external (for example a regulation or an order from someone else).**
    In my job I **have to** work from nine o'clock to five o'clock.
    (The obligation comes from "outside" the speaker. The speaker sees the obligation to work between nine o'clock and five o'clock as an external obligation.)

- **We use *must* to show something which the speaker sees as necessary.**
  I **must** do some more work. I have an exam tomorrow.
  (The obligation comes from the speaker. The speaker sees the obligation to do some more work as something which is necessary to do.)

mustn't / don't have to

- ***Mustn't* and *don't have to* have different meanings.**
  - **We use *mustn't* when we are not allowed to do something.**
    You **mustn't** copy during tests.
  - **We use *don't have to* when there is no necessity or obligation.**
    He **doesn't have to** invite them to his party.

Gerunds

- **A gerund is the *-ing* form of the verb. We use the gerund as the subject of a sentence.**
  Eating hamburgers and French fries is unhealthy.
  Swimming is fun.

Verb + *-ing* form

Subject	Verb	*-ing* form
I / you / he / she / it / we / you / they	love like enjoy prefer don't mind don't like hate	**swimming**

- **We use the verb + *-ing* form after a verb of preference such as *love*, *like*, *enjoy*, *prefer*, *don't mind*, *don't like*, and *hate*.**
  I love shopp**ing**, but I hate clean**ing** my room.
  I don't like rid**ing** my bike to school.

Word list

Housework
clean my room ____________
clean the bathroom ____________
do the cooking ____________
do the dusting ____________
do the grocery shopping ____________
do the ironing ____________
do the washing ____________
lay / clear the table ____________
load / unload the dishwasher ____________
make my bed ____________
take out the trash ____________
wash the dishes ____________

Student Book pp.20–22, p.23

Vocabulary

Housework

1 Match the verbs and phrases.

1 load	a the dishes
2 make	b the ironing
3 wash	c my bedroom
4 lay	d the dishwasher
5 do	e my bed
6 clean	f the table

2 Complete the phrases with the verbs in the box.

clean ~~clear~~ do do do take out

clear the table
1 ________ the bathroom
2 ________ the cooking
3 ________ the grocery shopping
4 ________ the trash
5 ________ the dusting

Grammar

have to
Affirmative and negative

3 Complete the sentences with the correct forms of *have to* and the verbs.

The dog *has to stay* (stay) in the yard. It can't come in the house. (✓)
1 We ________ (wash) the dishes every day. (✓)
2 Hyun ________ (study) for math tests. She's very good at math. (✗)
3 You ________ (finish) the project before the end of the month. (✗)
4 I ________ (leave) right now. Sorry! (✓)
5 Alak and Wasi ________ (go) to school tomorrow. (✗)
6 John ________ (get up) early today. (✓)

have to
Interrogative and short answers

4 Look at the chart. Write questions and short answers with *have to*.

	Amy	Ryan
make his / her bed	✓	✓
load the dishwasher	✓	✗
wash the dishes	✗	✗
take out the trash	✗	✓
lay the table	✓	✓
do the ironing	✗	✗

Amy / make her bed?
Does Amy have to make her bed?
Yes, she does.
1 Ryan / wash the dishes?
____
____
2 Amy / load the dishwasher?
____
____
3 they / lay the table?
____
____
4 Ryan / take out the trash?
____
____
5 they / do the ironing?
____
____

mustn't / don't (doesn't) have to

5 Complete the sentences with *mustn't*, *don't have to*, or *doesn't have to*.

We *don't have to* go to school on weekends.
1 Sam ________ take the dog for a walk. I took him this afternoon.
2 You ________ listen to music when you ride your bike.
3 We're having a surprise birthday party for Ben on Friday! You ________ tell him.
4 You ________ do the exercises now. You can do them for homework.
5 It's an exam! You ________ talk!
6 I ________ wash the dishes tonight! It's my brother's turn.

Gerunds

6 Complete the sentences with the gerund form of the verbs.

Doing the dusting is more boring than *washing* the dishes. (do / wash)

1 __________ a meal is cheaper than __________ in a café. (cook / eat)

2 __________ a book is more interesting than __________ TV. (read / watch)

3 __________ Chinese is more difficult than __________ English. (learn)

4 __________ English is easier than __________ English. (speak / write)

5 __________ is more exciting than __________. (skateboard / ski)

6 __________ by car is faster than __________ by train. (travel)

7 Write three sentences like the ones in exercise 6. Use the verbs in the box.

learn listen play read run send shop ~~sleep~~ swim travel

Sleeping is more exciting than learning math!

1 __________

2 __________

3 __________

Verb + *-ing* form

8 Look at the chart. Then write sentences.

love = ☺☺ like = ☺ don't mind = 😐
don't like = ☹ hate = ☹☹

	João	Kenji
cook	☺	☹☹
listen to music	☺	☺
go to the movies	☹	☺
do homework	☹	😐
read	☹	☺☺
get up early	😐	😐

João / cook *João likes cooking.*

1 Kenji / cook __________

2 Kenji / read __________

3 João and Kenji / listen to music __________

4 João and Kenji / get up early __________

5 João / go to the movies __________

6 Kenji / do homework __________

Round-up

9 Choose the correct answers.

Saturday – the best day of the week!

For 15-year-old Kelly Wright, Saturday is the best day of the week.

"I love weekends because I *(don't have to)* / mustn't go to school! Saturday is my favorite day. On Saturday mornings, I work at a home for rescued animals. I have [1]**to get up / getting up** at 6 a.m. When I get to work I [2]**have / must** to give the animals their food. I [3]**don't have to / mustn't** be late because the animals are always hungry in the morning. After that, there are lots of other jobs to do. I love [4]**playing / play** with the dogs but I hate [5]**wash / washing** them! I [6]**don't have to / mustn't** work in the afternoon. I usually hang out with my friends. We like [7]**going / go** to the mall. [8]**Shopping / Shop** is our favorite hobby! Some of my friends go out on Saturday evening, but I can't go with them because I have to be home by 8 p.m. They [9]**don't have to / mustn't** be home until 10 p.m. My parents are very strict. It isn't fair!"

10 Read the text again. Then answer the questions.

Why does Kelly love weekends?
Kelly loves weekends because she doesn't have to go to school.

1 What time does she have to get up on Saturday?

2 What does she have to do when she gets to work?

3 What does she love doing?

4 What does she hate doing?

5 What does she like doing with her friends on Saturday afternoon?

6 What is their favorite hobby?

7 Why can't Kelly go out with her friends on Saturday evening?

Asking for permission

1 Complete the dialogue with the phrases in the box.

~~can I go~~ have to do I'm sorry, you can't may I go to you can go

1

Jennifer Mom, can I go to Susan's house?
Mom ¹__________, Jennifer. You have to clean your room.
Jennifer But Mom we ²__________ our science project.
Mom Jennifer, your room is a mess!
Jennifer But doing my science project is more important.
Mom Clean your room first. Then ³__________ to Susan's house.
Jennifer Mom! I hate cleaning my room!
Mom Jennifer!

2

Kenny Miss Harper.
Miss Harper Yes, what is it Kenny?
Kenny ⁴__________ the bathroom, please?
Miss Harper Not now, Kenny. You have to wait.

2 Match the questions and answers.

1 Dad, can I go to Ruth's house this evening? c
2 Jade, can I borrow your blue T-shirt? ☐
3 Mom, I'm very hungry. Can I make a sandwich? ☐
4 Dad, I want to buy a magazine. Can you give me some money? ☐
5 Excuse me, Miss Yates. Can I put my bag on that chair? ☐
6 Can I borrow your MP3 player? ☐

a I'm sorry, you can't. It's in the washing machine.
b No, you can't. Put it under your desk.
~~c~~ No, you can't. You have to babysit your little brother. Mom and I are going out.
d No, you can't. We're having dinner soon.
e Sure. I'm not listening to it right now.
f OK. How much is it?

3 Complete the dialogues with the phrases in the box.

I'm sorry, you can't. I don't have any credit.
I'm sorry, you can't. I have to finish writing some e-mails.
No, you can't. I'm watching the news.
No, you can't, Olivia. Sit in front of Peter.
Sure. The coffee is there and the milk is in the refrigerator.
~~Sure, it's very cold in here.~~
Yes, of course. Put it under that desk.

A Can I close the window?
B Sure, it's very cold in here.

1 A May I sit next to Helen, Miss Lane?
B __________
2 A Can I watch the soccer game?
B __________
3 A Can I make some coffee?
B __________
4 A Can I use the computer?
B __________
5 A May I leave my school bag here?
B __________
6 A Can I use your cell phone?
B __________

Student Book p.22

Reading

1 Read the text. What is it about?

a Child labor in the U.S. today
b Child labor in Third World Countries
c Child labor in the U.S. in the past

I work downstairs in the kitchen.

In the U.S. in the 19th century many young children worked to support their families. Children worked in factories, farms, mines, or in the homes of rich families. Read about twelve-year-old Hannah Wheatley's life as a maid in Boston in 1832.

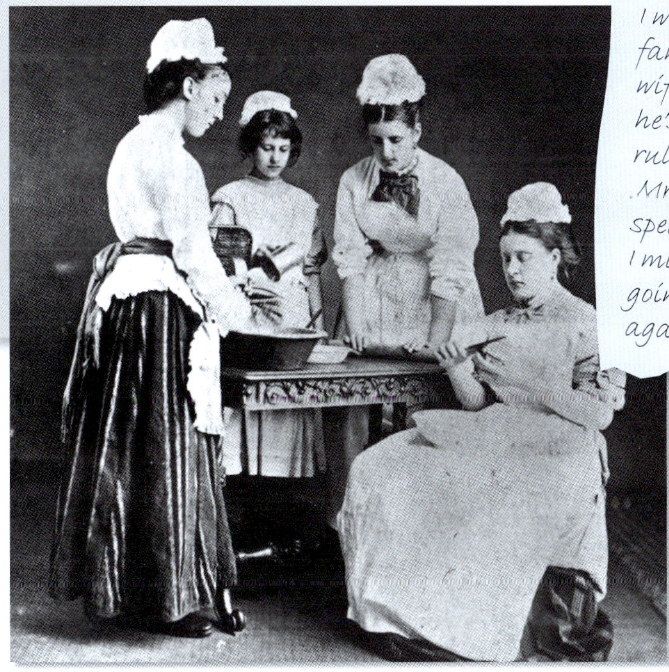

I start work at 5:30 a.m. and I finish at midnight. I have to clean the kitchen, wash the floors, and lay and clear the table in the dining room upstairs. I don't have to cook – Mrs. Harper, the cook, prepares the meals, but I have to help her and after every meal I have to wash the dishes. I hate washing the dishes – it takes a long time and everything has to be perfect. Last week I broke an expensive crystal glass and I had to pay for it.
I work downstairs in the kitchen most of the time. I don't see the family who live in the house – that's Mr. Henderson and his wife and children. I only see Mrs. Harper and Mr. Granger – he's the head servant – and the other servants. There are strict rules in the house. We must wear a uniform and we must call Mr. Granger "Sir" and Mrs. Harper "Ma'am". We can only speak when they ask a question.
I miss my family. I only go home one Sunday a month. I hate going back to the house to work, but the next day I'm happy again because I know I can send money to help my family.

2 Complete the factfile with information from the text.

My name: Hannah Wheatley
My age: [1] ____________
My occupation: [2] ____________
My employer's name: [3] ____________
I start work at: [4] ____________
I finish work at: [5] ____________
Jobs I have to do: clean the kitchen
[6] ____________
[7] ____________
[8] ____________
House rules: I have to call Mr. Granger "Sir" and Mrs. Harper "Ma'am".
My free days: [9] ____________

Writing

3 Imagine it is 1831 and you are a can washer in a factory in Boston. Invent details to complete the fact file.

My name: ____________
My age: ____________
My occupation: can washer
My employer's name: ____________
I start work at: ____________
I finish work at: ____________
Jobs I have to do: count cans, wash cans, put cans in boxes
Factory rules: I mustn't be late.
I mustn't speak while I'm working.
I have to ask for permission to go to the bathroom.
My free days: ____________

4 Write a short text about your job as a can washer. Use the information in exercise 3.

3 Grammar rules

be going to (1)
Affirmative

Full form	Short form
I **am going to** play	I**'m going to** play
you **are going to** play	you**'re going to** play
he **is going to** play	he**'s going to** play
she **is going to** play	she**'s going to** play
it **is going to** play	it**'s going to** play
we **are going to** play	we**'re going to** play
you **are going to** play	you**'re going to** play
they **are going to** play	they**'re going to** play

Subject +	*am* *are* *is*	*going to*	+ base form of the verb

1 We use *be going to* to:
- **talk about people's intentions.**
  She**'s going to** become an actor.
- **talk about things which people have decided to do in the future.**
  I**'m going to** play tennis tonight.

2 We usually use the short form of *be* with *be going to*.
They**'re going to** Sue's party on Saturday.

be going to
Negative

Full form
I **am not going to** play
you **are not going to** play
he **is not going to** play
she **is not going to** play
it **is not going to** play
we **are not going to** play
you **are not going to** play
they **are not going to** play

Short form
I **'m not going to** play
you **aren't going to** play
he **isn't going to** play
she **isn't going to** play
it **isn't going to** play
we **aren't going to** play
you **aren't going to** play
they **aren't going to** play

Subject +	*'m not* *aren't* *isn't*	*going to*	+ base form of the verb

- **We usually use the short form of *be* with *be going to*.**
  They **aren't going to** Sue's party on Saturday.

be going to
Interrogative and short answers

Interrogative form
Am I **going to** play?
Are you **going to** play?
Is he **going to** play?
Is she **going to** play?
Is it **going to** play?
Are we **going to** play?
Are you **going to** play?
Are they **going to** play?

Am *Are* *Is*	+ subject	*going to*	+ base form of the verb

Short answers	
Affirmative	**Negative**
Yes, I **am**.	**No,** I'**m not**.
Yes, you **are**.	**No,** you **aren't**.
Yes, he **is**.	**No,** he **isn't**.
Yes, she **is**.	**No,** she **isn't**.
Yes, it **is**.	**No,** it **isn't**.
Yes, we **are**.	**No,** we **aren't**.
Yes, you **are**.	**No,** you **aren't**.
Yes, they **are**.	**No,** they **aren't**.

Yes,	+ subject	*am / are / is*.
No,	pronoun +	*'m not / aren't / isn't*.

- **We usually use the short form of *be* with *be going to* in the negative short answer.**
  Are they **going to** Sue's party on Saturday?
  Yes, they **are**. / No, they **aren't**.

be going to (2)

- **We also use *be going to* to make predictions when there is something in the present which tells us about the future.**
  Look at the big, black clouds. It**'s going to** rain.
  It's late! My mom**'s going to** be angry!

Verb + infinitive / *-ing* form

Verb + infinitive		Verb + *-ing* form	
I **hope**		I **like**	
		I **love**	
I **want**	**to** fly.	I **hate**	
		I **don't mind**	fly**ing**.
I**'d like**		I **prefer**	
		I **enjoy**	

- **After some verbs we use the infinitive with *to* and after some verbs we use the *-ing* form.**
  I **hope to go** on vacation soon.
  She **wants to write** you an e-mail.
  We**'d like to leave** early because we're tired.
  I **enjoy playing** computer games.
  I **don't mind visiting** my grandma on the weekends.

Watch out!

Notice the difference between ***like*** and ***'d like***:
I like going to the mountains.
(*I often go to the mountains and I like it.*)
I'd like to go to the mountains.
(*In the future, I want to go to the mountains.*)

Word list

Personality
ambitious ________
bossy ________
confident ________
creative ________
friendly ________
hard-working ________
kind ________
lazy ________
organized ________
outgoing ________
patient ________
selfish ________
serious ________
shy ________
stubborn ________

Student Book pp. 32–33, p.35

Exercises

Vocabulary

Personality

1 Choose the correct answers.

Jason is really **selfish** / **bossy**. He always tells people what to do.

1 Don't be so **lazy** / **hard-working**! Get out of bed!
2 Wow. Did you paint that? You're very **stubborn** / **creative**.
3 Don't be **shy** / **confident**, Kelly. Just think about the play and forget the people in the theater.
4 Davi is very **outgoing** / **organized**. He likes meeting new people at parties.
5 Nina's very **kind** / **patient**. She helps the old people next door with their housework.
6 Lara is very **selfish** / **ambitious**. She never shares anything with anyone.

Grammar

be going to Affirmative and negative

2 Complete the e-mail from Jenny with the correct affirmative forms of *be going to* and the verbs in the box.

cook do have help learn listen ~~make~~ wear work

Hi Jess!
We're back from our vacation in Australia – here's a photo of me on Bondi Beach! My hair is shorter now and I *'m going to make* a lot of other changes in my life, too. I [1] ________ hard this year and I [2] ________ all my homework! I'm tired of all my CDs so I [3] ________ to different music this year, too.
My brother Billy and I [4] ________ a party before school starts. We [5] ________ Australian hats, Mom [6] ________ Australian food, and I [7] ________ her. Yes, I [8] ________ to cook this year as well!
See you soon,
Jenny

3 Complete the sentences. Use the correct negative forms of *be going to* and the phrases in the box.

buy it do it today ~~eat it~~ get up early play in the game read it

This cake is horrible! I *'m not going to eat it*.

1 This book is boring. I ________.
2 Naoto and Haruki don't like the band's new CD. They ________.
3 It's Sunday! We ________.
4 Rob isn't very well. He ________.
5 We have lots of history homework, but we ________.

4 Complete the sentences with the correct affirmative and negative forms of *be going to* and the verbs in the box.

~~drop it~~ jump pass the test score a goal win the race

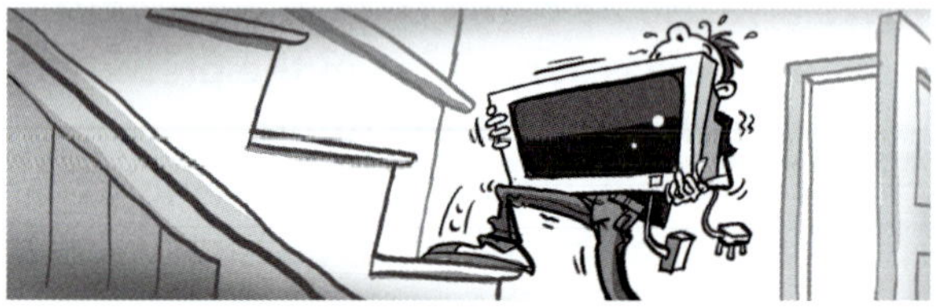

He *'s going to drop it*.

1 He ________

2 She ________

3 She ________

4 He ________

be going to
Interrogative and short answers

5 Complete the interview with the correct forms of *be going to*.

Pop Star Magazine interviews American singer Suzie Wu, from *The Tomahawks*.

PS Thanks for coming to talk to us, Suzie. How long are you going to stay (you / stay) in London?
Suzie For about ten days.
PS [1] ____________ (you / play) any concerts in South Korea?
Suzie No, we [2] ____________.
PS Really? What [3] ____________ (you / do) in Seoul?
Suzie I [4] ____________ (meet) some Korean musicians this weekend.
PS Wow. [5] ____________ (you / record) your next CD with them?
Suzie Yes, we [6] ____________.
PS I can't wait to hear it! And [7] ____________ (you / continue) recording when you go back to the U.S?
Suzie No, we [8] ____________. We're going to have a vacation.
PS Well, have a good time, Suzie. And thanks for talking to *Pop Star Magazine*.

Verb + infinitive / *-ing* form

6 Complete the sentences in the questionnaire. Check (✓) the sentences which are true for you.

What kind of person are you?

1 I don't mind waiting (wait) in line. ☐
2 I prefer ____________ (make) decisions quickly. ☐
3 I don't want ____________ (help) my parents with the housework. ☐
4 I'd like ____________ (write) stories. ☐
5 I hope ____________ (be) very rich one day. ☐
6 I love ____________ (tell) other people to do things. ☐
7 I enjoy ____________ (do) my homework ☐

Round-up

7 Complete the text with *be going to*, the infinitive with *to*, or the *-ing* forms of the verbs.

THE SECRETS OF SUCCESS

As teenagers we have to make a lot of decisions. What subjects are we going to study? What job [1] ____________ (we / do)? These are really important decisions and we don't want [2] ____________ (make) any mistakes! Here are Teen Life Magazine's secrets for a successful future.

Think about your personality
Personality helps you to decide what job is right for you. People with outgoing personalities love [3] ____________ (meet) lots of people in their jobs, but other people prefer [4] ____________ (have) quieter, more creative jobs. Would you like [5] ____________ (be) a doctor, an engineer, or an artist? What do you really like [6] ____________ (do)?

Try something new
Most young people enjoy [7] ____________ (sit) in front of the TV or a computer in their free time, but why not do something different sometimes? People with lots of hobbies and interests are usually more successful.

Don't forget your family and friends
Ambition is good because it helps us to work hard but very ambitious people can become selfish. We all hope [8] ____________ (be) rich and famous one day, but we mustn't forget our family and friends!

8 Read the text again. Then answer the questions.

What important decisions do teenagers have to make according to the article?
Teenagers have to decide what subjects they are going to study and what they are going to do.

1 Why is it important to think about your personality when you are choosing a job?
2 What do outgoing people like doing?
3 What do most young people enjoy doing in their free time?
4 What does the article say about people with lots of hobbies?
5 Why is ambition both a good and a bad thing?

Inviting people to do things

1 Complete the dialogue with the phrases in the box.

~~are you free~~ do you want to how about going I'd like to see I love going I'm busy let's do that would you like (x2)

1

Mark *Are you free* on Friday?
Linda Yes, I am.
Mark [1] ____________ to have dinner together?
Linda I'd love to, but I can't. [2] ____________ until 8 p.m.
Mark [3] ____________ to the movies at 9 p.m?
Linda Sure. [4] ____________ to the movies. [5] ____________ the new James Bond movie.
Mark Cool. I love action movies.

2

Jeff [6] ____________ to play tennis?
Maria No, thanks! I hate playing tennis! And it's going to rain! Look at the sky!
Jeff OK. [7] ____________ watch a DVD at my house?
Maria Cool. [8] ____________!

2 Match the questions and answers.

1 Are you free on Saturday evening? [e]
2 Would you like to go to a karaoke club on Friday afternoon? [ ]
3 Do you want to go to *The Rivals* concert on Tuesday evening? [ ]
4 How about staying at home this evening? [ ]
5 Do you want to go to the basketball game on Saturday morning? [ ]
6 Would you like to go shopping with me after school? [ ]

a No, thanks. I hate rock music.
b Cool. We can watch TV or play computer games.
c No, thanks. I'm not a big sports fan.
d Cool! Let's go to the shopping mall near Millennium Park.
e No, I'm not. I'm going to a Carla's birthday party.
f Yes, I'd love to – but I'm not a very good singer!

3 Write the dialogues in the correct order.

1

- Are you free on Tuesday night? [1]
- It starts at 8:30 p.m. Let's meet at my house at 7:30 p.m. [ ]
- I have an extra ticket for the *Metro* concert. Would you like to go? [ ]
- Yes, I am. Why? [ ]
- Sure. I love their new CD. What time does the concert start? [ ]

2

- I'm sorry, I can't. I have a piano lesson at 4 p.m. [ ]
- Sure. I'd love to. [ ]
- What time does it finish? [ ]
- Would you like to go to the movies on Saturday afternoon? [1]
- I'm meeting Greg and Ally for a pizza after the movie. Do you want to come? [ ]
- It finishes at 5 p.m. [ ]

4 Look at the poster. Then complete the dialogue.

A Are you free on [1] ____________?
B Yes, I am.
A Would you like to [2] ____________?
B Sure! [3] ____________.
A It starts at [4] ____________ at the Cadillac Palace.
B How much are the tickets?
A [5] ____________

Reading

1 Read the article. Find the name of two volunteer organizations.

1 ______________ 2 ______________

Volunteers in the U.S.

Every year thousands of American teenagers work as volunteers. They work with animals, protect the environment or help people in poor areas of the United States. In return, they learn important new skills. We spoke to two teenage volunteers.

"When I first came to Pine Ridge, I was very surprised. The houses in Pine Ridge are very old and many of them don't have electricity or water! A lot of people here don't have jobs so they're very poor. We're helping to repair their houses and we're painting the local school.
I think I was a bit selfish before I volunteered to work with *Schools Together*. I knew there were many poor people in America, but I never really thought about the problem. I'm meeting lots of really nice kids in Pine Ridge and I'm making some important decisions about my life too. I think I'm going to study medicine when I'm older and become a doctor."
Todd Billings, 14

"I'm doing voluntary work twice a week with a group called *Green Space*. They're working in the south side of the city and they're going to change some really ugly places into parks. I'm planting trees and picking up trash, painting walls, and doing lots of other things to help them.
I was a bit shy before I started, but now I'm meeting really nice kids from all over the city and I'm making some new friends. It's good fun, but we're all very tired at the end of the day and then I have to cycle home!"
Tina Martin, 14

2 Write the correct name *Todd* or *Tina*. Which volunteer ...?

1 was very surprised at first Todd
2 repairs houses ______________
3 volunteers twice a week ______________
4 works in the south side of the city ______________
5 is very tired at the end of the day ______________
6 is going to be a doctor ______________
7 was a bit selfish ______________
8 cycles to the project ______________

Writing

3 Imagine you are doing voluntary work. Answer the questions. Then use your answers to write a short account of your experience as a volunteer.

- What voluntary work are you doing?
- Where is the project?
- How do you get to the project? (walk, cycle, bus, train ...)
- What is difficult, fun, or interesting about the job?
- Do you have to get up early / work hard?
- What are you going to do tomorrow?

Volunteer now!
We have spaces on the following projects:

- Food Bank: Collect food for poor people in your neighborhood
- Animal Shelter: Take care of rescued animals
- Hospital Friends: Visit sick children in hospital

4 Grammar rules

will: future
Affirmative and negative

Affirmative	
Full form	**Short form**
I **will** leave	I**'ll** leave
you **will** leave	you**'ll** leave
he **will** leave	he**'ll** leave
she **will** leave	she**'ll** leave
it **will** leave	it**'ll** leave
we **will** leave	we**'ll** leave
you **will** leave	you**'ll** leave
they **will** leave	they**'ll** leave

Subject + | ***will* / *'ll*** | **+ base form of the verb**

Negative	
Full form	**Short form**
I **will not** leave	I **won't** leave
you **will not** leave	you **won't** leave
he **will not** leave	he **won't** leave
she **will not** leave	she **won't** leave
it **will not** leave	it **won't** leave
we **will not** leave	we **won't** leave
you **will not** leave	you **won't** leave
they **will not** leave	they **won't** leave

Subject + | ***will not* / *won't*** | **+ base form of the verb**

- **We use *will* to:**
  - **predict or suppose.**
    It**'ll be** great. The weather **will be** fine.
  - **talk about future facts.**
    They**'ll arrive** on the 11 a.m. bus.
  - **express decisions taken at the moment.**
    It's raining. I**'ll lend** you my umbrella.
  - **offer to do something at the moment or later.**
    Don't worry, I**'ll** help you with the math homework.
  - **make a request in the second person singular or plural.**
    Will you help me with these heavy bags?

will: future
Interrogative and short answers

Interrogative	
Will I leave?	**Will** it leave?
Will you leave?	**Will** we leave?
Will he leave?	**Will** you leave?
Will she leave?	**Will** they leave?

Will | **+ subject** | **+ base form of the verb**

Short answers	
Affirmative	**Negative**
Yes, I **will**.	**No,** I **won't**.
Yes, you **will**.	**No,** you **won't**.
Yes, he **will**.	**No,** he **won't**.
Yes, she **will**.	**No,** she **won't**.
Yes, it **will**.	**No,** it **won't**.
Yes, we **will**.	**No,** we **won't**.
Yes, you **will**.	**No,** you **won't**.
Yes, they **will**.	**No,** they **won't**.

Yes,* / *No, | **+ subject +** | ***will.* / *won't.***

will / *be going to*

1. **We can talk about the future using three different verb forms: *will* + base form of the verb, *be going to* + base form of the verb, and present progressive.**
2. **We use *will* + base form of the verb to talk about:**
   - **things we cannot control.**
     I think it**'ll be** sunny tomorrow.
     Airplanes **will fly** faster in the future.
   - **when we decide to do something at the moment of speaking.**
     We**'ll meet** you at the bus stop.
     I**'ll call** you back in a minute.
3. **We use *be going to* + base form of the verb to talk about:**
   - **intentions, things we have already decided to do.**
     I**'m going to read** this new book.
     We**'re going to go** swimming in the ocean on

vacation.

- **something in the present that tells us something about the future.**
  There's a lot of traffic. We**'re going to be** late for the bus.
  Look at those black clouds. It**'s going to rain**.

4 **We use the present progressive to talk about things that we arrange to do in the future.**
"What **are** you **doing** tonight?"
"**I'm having** dinner with Laura."

First conditional

Affirmative	
If we study, we**'ll** pass our exams.	
Hypothesis	**Consequence**
If we study,	we**'ll** pass our exams.

If	**+ subject +**	***simple present,***
subject +	***will / 'll***	**+ base form of the verb**

Negative	
If you don't play, the team **won't** win.	
Hypothesis	**Consequence**
If you don't play,	the team **won't** win.

***If* +**	**subject +**	***simple present,***
subject +	***will not / won't***	**+ base form of the verb**

1 **We use the first conditional to talk about future situations that the speaker thinks are probable.**
If she leaves before ten o'clock, she'll catch the bus.
(The speaker thinks it is probable that she will leave before ten o'clock and then catch the bus.)

2 **We make first conditional sentences with two parts: an *if*-clause (the hypothesis) and a main clause (the consequence).**

3 **We make the *if*-clause with *if* + subject + *the simple present* form of the verb + comma (,).**
If we **see** Victoria, we will tell her.

4 **We make the main clause with subject + *will / won't* + base form of the verb.**
If we see Victoria, we **will tell** her.

5 **We can put the *if*-clause at the beginning or end of a sentence. When the *if*-clause is at the beginning of a sentence, we put a comma (,) after it.**
If the weather **is** nice, we**'ll go** out.
We**'ll go** out if the weather **is** nice.

6 **We can also use imperatives in the main clause when we want to give orders.**
Stop working if you're tired.
Don't wear those shoes if you want to go walking in the mountains.

Word list

The weather
cloudy ____________
foggy ____________
raining ____________
snowing ____________
sunny ____________
windy ____________

Temperature
cold ____________
freezing ____________
hot ____________
mild ____________
warm ____________

Student Book pp.40–41, p.43

Vocabulary

The weather

1 Complete the map with the words in the box.

cloudy foggy raining
snowing ~~sunny~~ windy

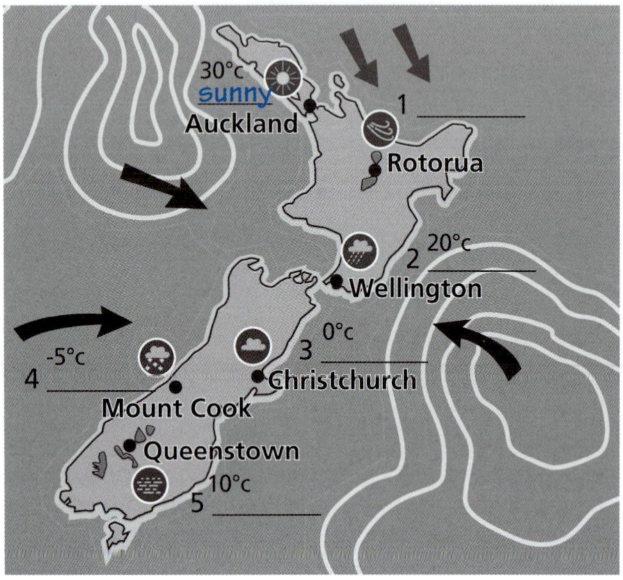

2 Match the cities to the adjectives.

1 Wellington — d
2 Queenstown
3 Christchurch
4 Mount Cook
5 Auckland

a freezing
b hot
c cold
d warm
e mild

Grammar

will: future
Affirmative and negative

3 Choose the correct answers.

Oh no! That was Mom's favorite clock! She **(won't)** / **will** be happy when she comes home!

1 They **won't** / **will** win the game. They're much better than the other team.
2 We **won't** / **'ll** have a really good time this weekend. We're going to the beach.
3 Don't worry, you **'ll** / **won't** fail the science test. You're good at science.
4 Bianca **will** / **won't** like this music. She doesn't listen to hip-hop.
5 Please tell me your secret. I **will** / **won't** tell anyone. I promise!

will: future
Interrogative and short answers

4 Complete the dialogues with the correct forms of the verbs in the box.

come do enjoy give stay take ~~win~~

A *Will they win the music competition?*
B No, I don't think they'll win the music competition. They're not very good.

1 A ________________
B Yes, he will. Paulo always takes his vacation in January.

2 A ________________
B No. Helen won't come to the party because she's busy.

3 A ________________
B No, he won't enjoy the movie. Jim's scared of horror movies.

4 A ________________
B Yes, the teacher will give us a test today.

5 A ________________
B No, my parents won't stay at my uncle's house. They're going to reserve a hotel.

6 A ________________
B Yes, Laura will do her school project. She's very hard-working.

will / *be going to*

5 Complete the sentences with *will* and *be going to*.

I *'m going to* call Lilly this afternoon. Maybe she *will* come to the park with us.

1 Sam ____________ join a band. Maybe he ____________ be famous one day.
2 We ____________ invite Laura and Chloe to our house, but I don't think Laura ____________ come – she never comes.
3 We hope the weather ____________ be nice this weekend because we ____________ have a picnic.
4 My parents ____________ take us to Hollywood this summer. Maybe we ____________ see a movie star!
5 I ____________ go to track and field practice now so I ____________ be very tired tonight.

First conditional

6 Match the sentence halves.

1 You'll have an accident … b
2 Danny will come with us tomorrow …
3 Will your parents be angry …
4 It's 2°C today. If you go out in a T-shirt, …
5 Will you go to the park tomorrow …
6 I'll help you with your English homework …

a if he isn't busy.
~~b~~ if you ride your bike like that.
c if the weather is nice?
d if you help me with my science project.
e you'll be cold.
f if you fail the exam?

7 Rewrite the sentences. Use the correct forms of the first conditional.

I don't want to be late. I must catch the eight o'clock bus.
If I don't catch the eight o'clock bus, I'll be late.

1 Don't skateboard in the street. You'll have an accident.
If you skateboard ______
______

2 Work hard and pass the exam.
If you ______
______

3 Don't watch that horror movie. You won't sleep very well.
If ______
______

4 Don't eat a lot of candy because you won't have nice teeth.
______
______

5 I hope the weather will be good tomorrow because I want to go to the beach.
______
______

Round-up

8 Read the text. Choose the correct answers.

Water world

Scientists predict that, in the next 100 years, the climate (will get) / is getting warmer. If that [1]**will happen / happens**, sea levels [2]**rise / will rise**. This [3]**will / won't** flood large areas of the world. At the same time the world's population [4]**will grow / growing** to ten billion people. So where [5]**we will / will we** all live?
Well, what about under the ocean? At the moment builders are building an underwater hotel near Dubai. *The Hydropolis* [6]**will be / is** the first underwater hotel in the world! The rooms will [7]**have / has** transparent walls so that you can watch the fish! There certainly won't be any underwater houses, schools, or stores in the near future. But, if the climate [8]**will continue / continues** to change, experts think that life under the ocean [9]**will become / becomes** a real possibility.

9 Are the sentences true or false? Correct the false statements.

Sea levels will rise because of global cooling.
False. Sea levels will rise because of global warming.

1 The world's population will be smaller in 100 years time.
______

2 Builders are building schools and stores under the ocean at the moment.
______

3 *The Hydropolis* will be an underwater hotel.
______

4 There will be underwater schools in the near future.
______

5 Life under the ocean won't become a real possibility.
______

Making offers

1 Complete the dialogues with the phrases in the box.

hot I'll drive I'll get I'll switch on I'll make ~~oh no!~~ thanks

1 A Oh no! It's going to rain and I don't have an umbrella!
B Don't worry, [1] ________ you home
A That's very kind of you, but it isn't far. I can walk.
B OK, [2] ________ you an umbrella.
A OK. Thanks.

2 A It's [3] ________ in here.
B Yes, it is. [4] ________ the air conditioning.
A Great. [5] ________

3 A I'm really hungry!
B There's some cheese in the refrigerator. [6] ________ you a sandwich if you want.
A Oh yes, please. Thanks.

2 Complete the dialogues with the words and phrases in the box.

carry them for you great help you ~~lend you some~~ make you a cup of tea please thanks that's kind of you

1 A Oh no! I don't have any money! I can't pay for the bus.
B I'll lend you some until tomorrow.
A [1] ________! Thanks.

2 A I'm thirsty! Is there any orange juice?
B No, but I'll [2] ________ if you want.
A No, [3] ________. I don't drink tea.

3 A These shopping bags are heavy!
B I'll [4] ________.
A [5] ________ but I have my car with me. It's over there!

4 A I don't understand this math problem.
B I'm good at math. I'll [6] ________ later if you want.
A Yes, [7] ________. Thanks.

3 Complete the dialogues with *I'll* and the words in the box.

buy / tickets get / the chessboard go / store make / beds ~~open / window~~ tell / them

A It's hot in here.
B I'll open a window.
A Thanks.

1 A Let's go to the Weezer concert next week.
B OK ________.
A Great! Thanks.

2 A The boys' room is a mess!
B ________.
A Oh, yes, please. Thanks.

3 A We need some milk.
B OK, ________.
A That's OK. I can go later.

4 A Oh no! We forgot to invite Matt and Sara to the party. Will they be at school tomorrow?
B Yes, I think so. ________ about it.
A OK. Thanks.

5 A I'm bored!
B Let's play a game. ________.
A No, thanks. That's boring, too!

4 Use the information to write short dialogues.

A is cold
B offers to make her a hot drink
A accepts the offer

A I'm cold.
B I'll make you a hot drink if you like.
A Yes, please. Thanks.

1 A says there's nothing on TV
B offers to get a DVD from the video store
A accepts the offer

2 A is hungry
B offers to make a snack
A refuses the offer and says she'll wait for lunch

3 A has a dentist's appointment and won't be at school tomorrow morning
B offers to tell the teacher
A accepts the offer

 Student Book pp.42

Reading

1 Match the titles to the paragraphs.

a Find a safe place b Watch the weather c What if you are outside?

Tornadoes (or "twisters") are the strongest winds on earth. They can occur in most parts of the world, but are most common in the U.S. in "Tornado Alley". The wind speed inside a tornado can be over 500 kilometers an hour. It is difficult to predict when or where tornadoes will happen, but it is possible to survive them. Here is a short guide.

Surviving tornadoes

1 ________________

TV weather reports will tell you if there's tornado weather in your area. Unfortunately, we only know a tornado is going to happen when it touches the ground. Most tornadoes happen between 3 p.m. and 7 p.m., so watch the sky at these times.

2 ________________

Prepare a tornado shelter in your house. This can be any downstairs room with strong walls and no windows. When a tornado comes, hide in this room. A tornado is very loud so you will hear it before it arrives. Don't leave the shelter when the sound stops. Stay there for 30 minutes in case the tornado returns.

3 ________________

It is terrifying to be outside in a tornado, but you'll probably survive if you don't panic. Never try to run when the tornado arrives because it can move very fast. Flying objects will hit you if you stand up or run, so stop and lie down. If you are in a car when a tornado hits, you will be safer outside the car. Tornadoes can pick up a car and objects can come through the windows. Tell your parents to stop the car, then get out and lie down.

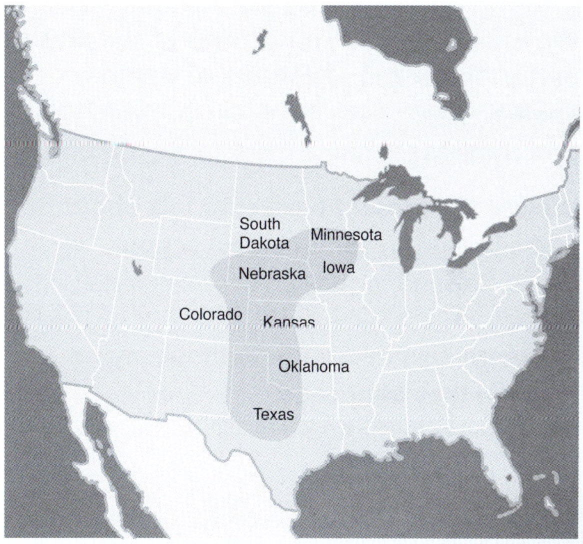

2 Read the text again. Then answer the questions.

1 What are twisters?
2 Why is it a good idea to watch the TV weather reports?
3 When do most tornadoes happen?
4 What kind of room is a good tornado shelter?
5 Why mustn't you try to run away from a tornado?
6 Why is it a bad idea to stay in a car?

Writing

3 Write a short text about the weather in your country. Include the following information:

- what the weather is like in summer and in winter
- what extreme weather conditions sometimes happens
- when extreme weather usually happens
- when and where the last extreme weather event happened

5 Grammar rules

Present perfect
Affirmative

Full form	Short form
I **have won**	I**'ve won**
you **have won**	you**'ve won**
he **has won**	he**'s won**
she **has won**	she**'s won**
it **has won**	it**'s won**
we **have won**	we**'ve won**
you **have won**	you**'ve won**
they **have won**	they**'ve won**

Subject + | ***have* ('*ve*)** / ***has* ('*s*)** | **+ past participle**

1 We make the present perfect with the simple present form of the auxiliary verb *have* + the past participle of the main verb.
They **have bought** a new computer.

2 We usually use the short forms of the present perfect in spoken and informal written English.
He**'s come** to the movie theater with his sister.

3 We use the present perfect to talk about:
- **the present result of a past action.**
  I**'ve finished** my homework. I can watch TV now.
- **experiences in our life without saying when they happened.**
  I**'ve been** to Canada.

Present perfect
Negative

Full form	Short form
I **have not won**	I **haven't won**
you **have not won**	you **haven't won**
he **has not won**	he **hasn't won**
she **has not won**	she **hasn't won**
it **has not won**	it **hasn't won**
we **have not won**	we **haven't won**
you **have not won**	you **haven't won**
they **have not won**	they **haven't won**

Subject + | ***have not* (*haven't*)** / ***has not* (*hasn't*)** | **+ past participle**

1 We make the present perfect with the simple present form of the auxiliary verb *have* + *not* + the past participle of the main verb.
We **have not washed** the dishes.

2 We usually use the short forms of the present perfect in spoken and informal written English.
You **haven't switched** off the light.

Past participles

1 We make the past participle of regular verbs by adding *-ed* to the base form of the verb.

Regular verbs		
Base form	Simple past	Past participle
finish	finish**ed**	finish**ed**
play	play**ed**	play**ed**
watch	watch**ed**	watch**ed**

2 Remember the spelling variations:
- **when the verb ends in *-e*, we only add *-d*.**
  live – live**d**
- **when the verb ends in a vowel and then a consonant, we double the last consonant and then add *-ed*.**
  stop – sto**pped** plan – pla**nned**
- **when the verb ends in a vowel and then the letter *-y*, we replace *-y* with an *-i* and then add *-ed*.**
  study – stud**ied**

3 The past participle of irregular verbs changes for each verb. There are no rules to form the past participles. Look at the irregular verb list on the inside back cover and try to learn them.

been / gone

1 **We use the present perfect of *be* (*have been* / *has been*) to say that someone went to a place and then returned.**
Alan **has been** to China. He really liked it.
(*Alan went to China. Now he is at home.*)

2 **We use the present perfect of *go* (*have gone* / *has gone*) to say that someone went to a place and they are still there.**
Maria **has gone** to the park. She'll come back soon.
(*Maria went to the park. She is at the park now.*)

Present perfect
Interrogative and short answers

Interrogative	
Have I **won**?	**Has** it **won**?
Have you **won**?	**Have** we **won**?
Has he **won**?	**Have** you **won**?
Has she **won**?	**Have** they **won**?

Have / Has	**+ subject pronoun +**	**past participle**

Short answers	
Affirmative	**Negative**
Yes, I **have**.	**No,** I **haven't**.
Yes, you **have**.	**No,** you **haven't**.
Yes, he **has**.	**No,** he **hasn't**.
Yes, she **has**.	**No,** she **hasn't**.
Yes, it **has**.	**No,** it **hasn't**.
Yes, we **have**.	**No,** we **haven't**.
Yes, you **have**.	**No,** you **haven't**.
Yes, they **have**.	**No,** they **haven't**.

Yes,	**+ subject pronoun +**	***have / has.***
No,		***haven't / hasn't.***

- **We make the present perfect interrogative with *Have / Has* followed by the subject pronoun and the past participle of the verb.**
"**Have** you **traveled** by airplane?" "**Yes,** I **have**."
"**Has** Zoe **done** a parachute jump?" "**No,** she **hasn't**."

ever / never

1 ***Ever* means "in your life". We use *ever* in interrogative sentences between the subject pronoun and the past participle.**
Have you **ever** visited Chicago?
Has she **ever** eaten Greek food?

2 ***Never* means "not in your life". We use *never* in affirmative sentences between *have / has* and the past participle.**
They've ***never*** met a famous person.
He's ***never*** visited Colombia.

Present perfect / Simple past

1 **The present perfect and simple past do not have the same uses or meaning.**

2 **We use the simple past to talk about a completed past action. We also usually use the simple past with a past time expression which says when something happened (for example, *yesterday*, *a year ago*, *last Monday*, *in 2008*).**
I **went** to Mexico **last summer**.

3 **We use the present perfect to talk about the present result of a past action, or about an experience that happened in our lifetime, but we do not specify when it happened.**
I **have had** lunch. I can't go swimming now.
Have you **ever been** to Tokyo?

Word list

Exciting experiences
do a parachute jump ____________
fly in an airplane ____________
go camping ____________
go scuba diving ____________
meet a famous person ____________
ride a roller coaster ____________
stay in a hotel ____________
travel abroad ____________
watch a soccer game ____________

Student Book pp. 54–55, p.57

Vocabulary

Exciting experiences

1 Match the sentences with the phrases in the box.

~~do a parachute jump~~ go scuba diving ride a roller coaster stay in a hotel travel abroad watch a soccer game

Don't look down when you jump out of the airplane!
do a parachute jump

1 We saw some amazing fish.
______

2 We went to Mexico last summer – we caught a ferry from Cancún to Isla Mujeres. It was great.
______

3 I was really scared when we went fast. We traveled at 70 km/h!
______

4 It was great when my team scored a goal!
______

5 There was a swimming pool and the food was great. We were there five nights.
______

Grammar

Present perfect
Affirmative and negative

2 Complete the sentences with the correct present perfect forms of the verbs in the box.

~~buy~~ clean not come not have not use see start

Sally *has bought* a new MP3 player. It's cool!

1 Matt's hungry. He ______ lunch.
2 You've been on the Internet all evening and I ______ the computer all day!
3 I ______ that movie. It's great!
4 We're late! The concert ______.
5 Ayame and Hayate ______ to school today. Are they on vacation?
6 I ______ my room. Can I go to Jay's house?

been / gone

3 Rewrite the sentences with present perfect and *been / gone*.

England is a really nice place, but I'm happy to be back home.
I *'ve been to England.*

1 The movie was exciting, but the movie theater seats were dirty.
We ______.
2 Lucy's at Maria's house. She'll be back later.
Lucy ______.
3 My cousin Ricardo studies in Boston.
Ricardo ______.
4 Look at this e-mail. My brother's having a good time in Rome.
My brother ______.
5 What did you buy at the shopping mall?
You ______.

Present perfect
Interrogative and short answers

4 Complete the dialogue with questions and short answers.

Mom (you / lose / something?) *Have you lost something?*
Angie Yes, *I have*. (you / see / my MP3 player?) [1] ______
Mom No, [2] ______. (you / leave / it at school?) [3] ______
Angie No, [4] ______. I saw it this afternoon.
Mom (you / look / in your room?) [5] ______
Angie Yes, [6] ______. It's not there.
Mom (you / ask / Dad?) [7] ______
Angie No, [8] ______. (he / come / home?) [9] ______
Mom Yes, [10] ______. He's in the yard.
Angie Hi, Dad. (you / seen / my MP3 player?) [11] ______
Dad Er, yes, [12] ______. Sorry Angie. Do you want it back?

ever / never

5 Complete the dialogue with present perfect and *ever* or *never*.

Mi-Cha Hi. Are you an actor?
Dan No, I'm a stunt man. I'm going to jump from that train.
Mi-Cha Really? Have you ever jumped (you / jump) from a moving train before?
Dan No, I [1] ______________ (do) this stunt before.
Mi-Cha [2] ______________ (you / be) scared before a stunt?
Dan No, I [3] ______________ (feel) very scared because I [4] ______________ (have) an accident.
Mi-Cha You're very brave. [5] ______________ (you / fall) off a horse?
Dan Yeah, lots of times … in cowboy movies.
Mi-Cha Wow! [6] ______________ (you / jump) out of an airplane?
Dan Yes, I have. I was a skydiver in *Live too fast*.
Mi-Cha The Nathan Harker movie? Cool! [7] ______________ (you / meet) him?
Dan Of course. Nathan and I are good friends.

Present perfect / Simple past

6 Complete the dialogue with the correct forms of the present perfect or simple past.

A Have you ever seen (you / ever / see) Mikey Sno in concert?
B Yes, I have. He came (come) to Da Nang last year.

1 A [1] ______________ (you / call) Tom today?
B Yes, I [2] ______________. I [3] ______________ (call) him about thirty minutes ago.

2 A Jake [4] ______________ (not / be) at school this morning and it's nearly lunchtime. Do you know where he is?
B Yes, he's in the U.S. with his family. He [5] ______________ (leave) yesterday.

3 A [6] ______________ (you / ask) Mrs. Asari about the school trip?
B No, I [7] ______________. I [8] ______________ (go) to her classroom at eleven o'clock, but she wasn't there.

Round-up

7 Complete the text with the correct forms of the present perfect or simple past.

Man vs. Wild
by Luke Walters

My favorite celebrity is Bear Grylls. He's an adventurer and an explorer. He has been (be) all over the world and he [1] ______________ (do) some amazing things! He [2] ______________ (write) three books about his adventures and now he presents a TV series about how to survive in the wild.

Grylls [3] ______________ (be) born in the U.K. in 1974. He [4] ______________ (learn) to sail a boat when he was very young. As a child he also [5] ______________ (love) climbing and he became famous when he [6] ______________ (climb) Mount Everest at the age of 23!

Grylls [7] ______________ (visit) the freezing Arctic and the hot rainforests of the Amazon. On his TV show, *Man vs. Wild*, he [8] ______________ (try) a lot of exciting things. Last year he [9] ______________ (do) hundreds of parachute jumps, [10] ______________ (fight) an alligator and [11] ______________ (eat) snakes!

I [12] ______________ (never / do) anything exciting, but I'd like to travel one day. I always watch Bear Grylls on TV and I've learned a lot. I'm almost ready for adventure!

8 Write questions. Then answer the questions.

Where / be / Bear Grylls / born?
Where was Bear Grylls born? He was born in the U.K.

1 Why / he / become / famous?
____

2 What incredible places / he / visit?
____

3 What / he / do / on his TV show last year?
____

4 Luke / ever do / anything exciting?
____

Booking an activity

1 **Complete the dialogue with the phrases in the box.**

> and are you all over fifteen? ~~can I help you?~~
> have you been here before?
> how many people are there? is that OK?
> what's your name and cell number
> when do you want to book the lane for?

Receptionist	Hello, Brooklyn Bowl. Can I help you?
Rick	Yes, please. I'd like to book a bowling lane.
Receptionist	1 ________________
Rick	No, I haven't.
Receptionist	OK, 2 ________________, please?
Rick	It's Rick Nelson and my cell is 434-555-6328.
Receptionist	And 3 ________________
Rick	Saturday at 3 p.m., please.
Receptionist	OK – Saturday 10th at 3 p.m. 4 ________________
Rick	Three.
Receptionist	5 ________________
Rick	Yes, we are.
Receptionist	That'll be $30 for the lane and $4 each for shoe rental. 6 ________________
Rick	Yeah, that's fine.
Receptionist	OK. I've booked that for you.
Rick	That's great. Thanks. Bye.

2 **Write the dialogue in the correct order.**

B Twelve. ☐
A OK – Tuesday 22nd December at 11:30 a.m. How many people are there? ☐
B Yes, it's Pedro Williams and my cell number is 786-350-4911. ☐
A OK. Can I have your name and cell number, please? ☐
A That'll be $60 for the court. ☐
B For 11:30 a.m. tomorrow. ☐
A Hello. Can I help you? 1
B OK. Thanks. Bye. ☐
B Yes, we are. ☐
A Thank you, Pedro. And when do you want the basketball court for? ☐
B Yes, please. I'd like to book a basketball court, please. ☐
A That's fine. And are you all over thirteen? ☐

3 **Read your friend's note. Then complete the dialogue with the receptionist and answer the questions.**

> Hey there!
> There's a new sports center in Hudson Street. Let's go and see it! I'm free at 2 p.m. on Saturday.
> Why don't we play tennis?
> Leo
> P.S. If you're free, can you book the tennis court?

Receptionist	Hello. Can I help you?
You	Yes, please. I'd like to book a tennis court.
Receptionist	Have you been here before?
You	1 ________________
Receptionist	OK. What's your name and cell number, please?
You	2 ________________
Receptionist	When do you want to book the court for?
You	3 ________________
Receptionist	How many people are there?
You	4 ________________
Receptionist	Are you both over fourteen?
You	5 ________________
Receptionist	OK, that'll be $30 for an hour. Is that OK?
You	6 ________________
Receptionist	OK. I've booked that for you. Goodbye. Have a nice day.

4 **You want to go skateboarding. Look at the advertisement. Decide what time you'd like to go and who you'd like to go with. Call the skatepark to book a time. Write the dialogue you have with the receptionist.**

> **Avalon Skatepark**
> **Opening times:** Sunday – Thursday 11 a.m. – 8:30 p.m.
> Saturday 11 a.m. – 10:30 p.m.
> **Phone:** 843-750-7625
> **1790, 29th Avenue East, Myrtle Beach, SC 29576**

Receptionist	Hello, Avalon Skatepark. Can I help you?
You	Yes, I'd like to …

 Student Book p.56

Reading

1 Read the webpage. Then complete the chart.

What?	*Teen survival camp*
For who?	1 ________
Where?	2 ________
When?	3 ________
How long?	4 ________

2 Read the webpage again. Then answer the questions.

1 How many survival camps has Isaac been on?
2 What has he learned to do?
3 What did he think of the night walk that he did last year?
4 When did Holly go on the survival camp?
5 What was her favorite activity?

SURVIVOR

HOME CAMPS ABOUT US FAQs BLOG Search

Teen survival camps

Have you ever slept outdoors?
Have you ever camped without food or water?
Have you ever looked for food in a forest?

If you're between the age of fourteen and seventeen and you're looking for adventure, you'll find it at our Teen Survival Camps. The two-week camps take place every July and August in the Siskiyou Mountains in northern California. We take small groups of students (no more than eight people per group) and teach them basic survival skills. Each camp is full of fun, excitement, and experiences that you have never had before!

What students have said about the Teen Survival Camp:

"I've been on two survival camps and they've changed my life! I've never done anything so cool before! I've learned to make a fire, build a camp, and find food in the wild. I've even learned how to use the sun to get clean water! Last year we went on a night walk and we had to cross a forest without a map. It was awesome! You have to try it!" *Isaac, 17*

"It's the best camp I've ever been on and I've never learned so much in two weeks! I only went last month, but I'm already planning to go again next year! The people were great and I loved everything about it. My favorite thing was cooking over the campfire in the evening. Go for it!" *Holly, 16*

Writing

3 Imagine that you are at the Teen Survival Camp. It's Wednesday evening of the first week. Look at the calendar of events and then write an e-mail to your best friend. Say:

- what you think of the camp
- some of the things you've done so far
- what you did yesterday
- what the people are like
- what the food is like

This week's events

Monday	a.m. Build the camp site! Choose an area for cooking, sleeping, washing, etc. p.m. look for food in the forest Make a fire and cook the food! Sleep outdoors.
Tuesday	a.m. Walk to the river and build a raft Learn how to catch fish p.m. Night walk under the stars. Sleep in the forest!
Wednesday	a.m. Learn how to find signs of animals p.m. Learn how to climb mountainous areas

6 Grammar rules

Present perfect + *already*

Subject +	*have* ('ve) *has* ('s)	+ *already*	+ past participle

1 We use *already* to talk about something happening sooner than we expected.
I**'ve already seen** Valeria today.

2 We usually use *already* in affirmative sentences.
We**'ve already told** them to arrive at 8 p.m.

3 *Already* comes between the auxiliary verb (*have* / *has*) and the past participle.
She**'s already paid** for her pizza.

Present perfect + *yet*

Subject +	*have not* (*haven't*) *has not* (*hasn't*)	+ past participle	+ *yet*
Have / *Has*	+ subject	+ past participle	+ *yet*

1 We use *yet* to talk about something we are expecting to happen.
They **haven't moved** into the new house **yet**.

2 We usually use *yet* in negative and interrogative sentences.
Monica **hasn't taken** out the trash **yet**.
Has your brother **finished** high school **yet**?

3 *Yet* comes at the end of a sentence or question.
Have you **been** to see Nick at the hospital **yet**?

Present perfect + *just*

Subject +	*have* ('ve) *has* ('s)	+ *just*	+ past participle
Have / *Has*	+ subject	+ *just*	+ past participle

1 We use *just* to talk about something that happened a very short time ago.
I**'ve just received** an e-mail from Ben.

2 We use *just* in affirmative and interrogative sentences.
Clare **has just called**.
Has Tom **just left**?

3 *Just* comes before the past participle in affirmative and interrogative sentences.
Have Simon and Emma **just had** lunch?

Present perfect + *for* / *since*

1 We use the present perfect with *for* or *since* to describe an action which started in the past and continues until the present.

Dragon Tamers **has been** on the bestseller list **for** six months.
I**'ve known** Mateo **for** two years.
I**'ve been** a writer **since** I was fifteen years old.
She **has been** my best friend **since** we started high school.

2 We use *for* with a period of time. We use *for* to talk about the length of the period of time.

They**'ve worked** in Fortaleza **for** four years.

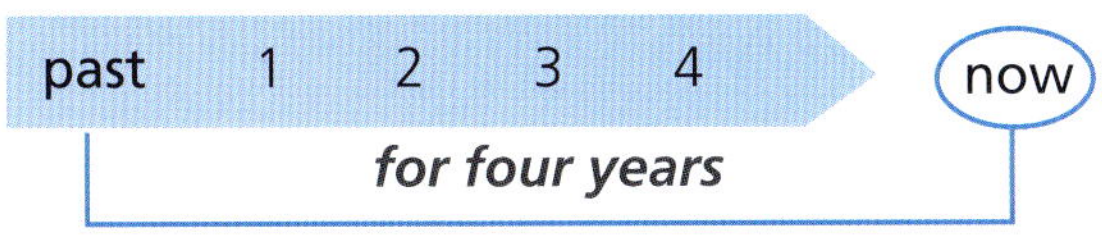

They've worked in Fortaleza **for four years**.

3 We can use the following time expressions with *for* in:

- ***for* + number of days – *for two days***
  Sal's gone to the city **for two days**.
- ***for* + number of weeks – *for three weeks***
  I've been on vacation **for three weeks**.
- ***for* + number of months – *for eight months***
  We've had a pet dog **for eight months**.
- ***for* + number of years – *for ten years***
  They've lived in Illinois **for ten years**.
- ***for* + expression**
  I've been in Manaus **for a while**.
  (*A short time, but we don't know exactly how long.*)
  I've been in Manaus **for a long time**.
  (*A long time, but we don't know exactly how long.*)

4 We use *since* with a point in time. We use *since* to talk about the beginning of a period of time.

We**'ve been** in Cali **since** Tuesday.

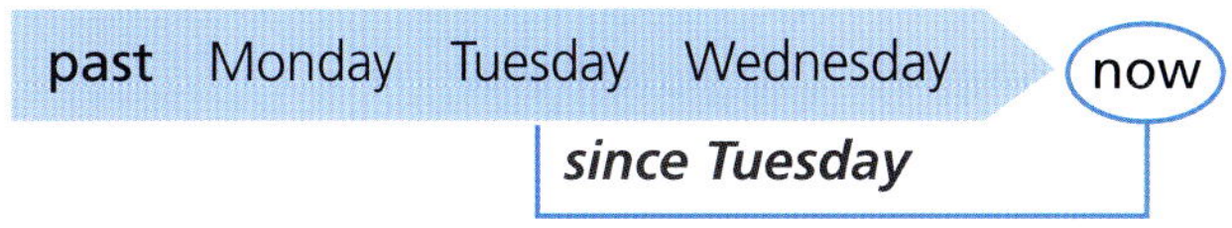

We've been in Cali **since Tuesday**.

5 We can use the following time expressions with *since*:

- ***since* + time – *since two o'clock***
  I've watched TV **since two o'clock**.
- ***since* + yesterday – *since yesterday***
  I haven't seen Vilma **since yesterday**.
- ***since* + day – *since Thursday***
  It's rained **since Thursday**.
- ***since* + month – *since May***
  We've had a car **since May**.
- ***since* + year – *since 2009***
  They've studied English **since 2009**.

Word list

Books
autobiography ____________
biography ____________
detective story / crime story ____________
fantasy story ____________
horror story ____________
love story ____________
science fiction story ____________
spy story ____________

6 Exercises

Vocabulary

Books

1 Complete the sentences.

I never read horror stories. I can't sleep after I read them.

1 It's a ______________ story about aliens from Mars.
2 I've read a lot of James Bond ______________ stories.
3 In this ______________ story, a man robs a bank.
4 It's a great ______________ story about dragons and wizards.
5 It's a ______________ about the life of Nelson Mandela.
6 This ______________ story is very romantic.
7 Many famous people have written about their life in an ______________.

Grammar

Present perfect + *yet* and *already*

2 Complete the dialogues with questions and answers. Use the present perfect and *yet*.

A Have you finished your project yet? (you / finish / your project?)
B No, I haven't started it yet. (I / not / start / it)

1 A Erin, ______________ (you / send the e-mail to Mary?)
B No, ______________ (I / not / switch on / the computer)
2 A ______________ (Tom / get up?)
B No, ______________ (he / not / wake up)
3 A ______________ (you / buy / the concert tickets?)
B No. ______________ (you / not / give / me the money)
4 A ______________ (they / have / their exam results?)
B ______________ (they / not / see / them)

3 Complete the sentences with the present perfect forms of the verbs and *already*.

I know about the test. Sofia has already told (tell) me.

1 That's a really good book. I ______________ (read) it twice.
2 Our homework was easy. We ______________ (finish) it.
3 Kasia doesn't want to see the James Bond movie. She ______________ (see) it.
4 Pedro can tell you all about the museum because he ______________ (visit) it.
5 I'm not going to call Rocio because I ______________ (send) her an e-mail.
6 Why do you want to take another photo of me? You ______________ (take) three!
7 Mom bought my baby brother a new toy, but he ______________ (break) it.

4 Complete the dialogue with *yet* or *already*.

Kris: Hi Pao! Oh … Zorro. I've already read that – it's a great book. Do you like it?
Pao: Well, I haven't finished it [1]______________, but it's very exciting.
Kris: How much have you read?
Pao: I've [2]______________ finished the first part.
Kris: Has Zorro traveled to Spain [3]______________?
Pao: Yes, he has. He's [4]______________ been there and come back to California.
Kris: Has he met Rafael Moncada [5]______________?
Pao: Yes, they've [6]______________ had a fight, but Rafael hasn't discovered who Zorro is [7]______________ because of his mask. But hey, don't tell me the ending. I haven't read that bit [8]______________!

Present perfect + *just*

5 Complete the sentences with *just* and the present perfect forms of the verbs in the box.

~~have~~ leave paint see wash win

A Are you thirsty?
B No, we've just had some water.

1 A Was that wall always that color?
B No. I ______________ it.

2 A Is Steve at school?
B No, he ______________.

3 A I can't find my cell phone.
B I ______________ it. It's in the living room.

4 A Why are you so happy?
B Corinthians ______________ the game!

5 A Why is your hair wet?
B I ______________ it.

Present perfect + *for* / *since*

6 Complete the sentences with *for* or *since*.

Where are you? I've been outside the movie theater for an hour.

1 We haven't seen Beth ______________ two months.

2 Mick's been on vacation in the U.S. ______________ last month.

3 She's studied English ______________ elementary school.

4 Kerri has known Andy ______________ five years.

5 I've played tennis ______________ three years. I love it!

6 My sister hasn't spoken to me ______________ last week when I broke her MP3 player!

Round-up

7 Complete the e-mail with *already*, *yet*, *just*, *for*, or *since*.

Hi, Sue
How are you? I'm sorry I haven't written for a few weeks, but I've been very busy. How are things in your new home in Hawaii? Everybody here in Minneapolis has missed you [1] ______________ you left. Have you started your new school [2] ______________? Have you made any new friends? Marcy says you've [3] ______________ forgotten all your old friends, but I know that isn't true! Nothing has changed here in Minneapolis – it's cold and boring as usual! But Becky is really excited at the moment because she's [4] ______________ won her black belt in Tae Kwon Do. Becky, Marcy, and I have decided to visit you next summer in Hawaii! We've [5] ______________ started planning the trip! I went to soccer practice last night and all the girls say "Hi!" We haven't won a game [6] ______________ weeks and weeks – [7] ______________ you left in fact!
OK. I have to finish now. *CSI Miami* has started and I don't want to miss it. Have you finished watching the first series on DVD [8] ______________? It's cool, right? I want to marry Adam Rodriguez!
Love,
Eva

8 Read the e-mail again. Then correct the mistakes in the sentences.

Eva has written to Sue every week.
Eva hasn't written to Sue for a few weeks.

1 Everybody has missed Sue since she left Hawaii.
____

2 Everything has changed in Minneapolis.
____

3 Becky has just won a yellow belt in judo.
____

4 Becky, Marcy, and Eva haven't started planning their trip to Hawaii.
____

5 Eva's soccer team has won all its games since Sue left.
____

6 *CSI Miami* has already finished and Eva has missed it.
____

Buying presents / souvenirs

1 Complete the dialogue with the phrases in the box.

> ~~can I help you?~~ here you are
> I'm looking for a present it's a bestseller
> there's a sale at the moment
> what kind of books

Salesclerk	Good morning. *Can I help you?*
Julia	Yes, please. [1] ____________ for my dad. I'd like to get him a book.
Salesclerk	Well, [2] ____________ does he read?
Julia	He loves crime stories.
Salesclerk	Has he read *The Scarpetta Factor* by Patricia Cornwell? [3] ____________.
Julia	Yes, he's already read it. He loved it.
Salesclerk	What about *Southern Cross* then? It's by the same writer. I've just finished it. It's great!
Julia	Cool! I think he'd like that. How much does it cost?
Salesclerk	It's $10, but [4] ____________. There's a 10% discount so that's $9.
Julia	Great. I'll take it. [5] ____________.
Salesclerk	Here's your change and your receipt.
Julia	Thanks.

2 Reorder the dialogue.

Dylan	Yes. I'm looking for a present for my sister. I'd like to get her a CD.	☐
Dylan	Thanks. Bye.	☐
Salesclerk	What about Rihanna's new CD?	☐
Salesclerk	Here's the receipt and your change. She can change it if she doesn't like it.	☐
Dylan	She's already bought it.	☐
Dylan	Great idea. I'll take it. How much is it?	☐
Salesclerk	Does she like the Black Eyed Peas? They have a new CD.	☐
Dylan	She usually listens to pop music but I don't like it. Do you have any ideas?	☐
Salesclerk	Hello! Can I help you?	1
Salesclerk	It's $10.99.	☐
Dylan	Here you are.	☐
Salesclerk	What kind of music does she like listening to?	☐

3 Complete the dialogue with the phrases in the box.

> but there's a sale at the moment so it's only $9.99 ~~can I help you?~~
> here's your change and your receipt.
> is this OK? that's $11.49. what size is she?
> which one would you like?
> would you like it wrapped as a gift?

Salesclerk	Hello. *Can I help you?*
Anh	Yes, I'd like to buy a T-shirt as a present for my friend, please.
Salesclerk	[1] ____________
Anh	How much is the one with the big apple on it?
Salesclerk	It's normally $14.99, [2] ____________
Anh	What sizes do you have?
Salesclerk	There's small, medium, or large. [3] ____________
Anh	She's a bit bigger than me. I think she's a size medium.
Salesclerk	Here you are. [4] ____________
Anh	OK, I'll take it.
Salesclerk	We sell gift bags and they're $1.50 each. [5] ____________
Anh	OK, I'll take a gift bag, too.
Salesclerk	[6] ____________
Anh	Here you are.
Salesclerk	Thanks. [7] ____________

Reading

"His name's Bond ... James Bond"

Who created the character of James Bond?

The British writer Ian Fleming created James Bond in his 1953 novel *Casino Royale*. He wrote a series of books about the secret agent between 1953 and 1966. The books have sold more than eighteen million copies in many different languages.

What is James Bond's code number?

His code number is 007. The prefix 00 means that James Bond can kill anyone without any problems. Bond takes this code name from the first novel, *Casino Royale*, when he killed two enemies. He has killed more than 150 villains since!

How does he defeat his enemies?

He uses his intelligence, strength, and high-tech weapons and devices. In the early stories these were guns or explosives that looked like everyday objects (a watch or a pen for example). In later stories the devices became more sophisticated and included x-ray glasses and a jetpack.

How many James Bond movies have there been?

There have been 22 official James Bond movies. The first movie was *Dr. No* in 1962 starring Sean Connery. The Bond movies are the second most successful series of movies in the history of cinema. (The most successful is the Harry Potter series.) In fact, about half of the world's population has seen a James Bond movie at the movies, on TV, or on DVD.

How many actors have played the part of James Bond?

Six actors have played the part of James Bond. The current Bond is English actor Daniel Craig, but most people's favorite Bond is the original – Sean Connery.

1 Read the article and find the following:

- James Bond's code number
  1 ________________
- the name of the first James Bond movie
  2 ________________
- the name of the actor who plays James Bond in the most recent movies 3 ________________

2 Read the article again. Are the sentences true or false? Correct the false sentences.

Ian Fleming wrote the first James Bond book in 1966.
False. Ian Fleming wrote the first James Bond book in 1953.

1 James Bond's code is 007 because he killed seven enemies in the first novel.
2 James Bond has killed more than 150 villains.
3 James Bond used everyday objects to fight his opponents in the early stories.
4 The Bond movies are the most successful series of movies in movie history.
5 About 75% of the world's population has seen a James Bond movie.
6 Six actors have played the part of James Bond.
7 Sean Connery plays James Bond in the most recent movies.

Writing

3 Write a paragraph about a character from a book or a movie that you like. Think about the following:

- Who is the character?
- What is he / she like? (funny, intelligent, romantic, a superhero ...)
- Who created the character?
- Has the character been in movies, TV shows, comics?
- Why do you like this character?

7 Grammar rules

Past progressive
Affirmative and negative

Affirmative	
I **was playing**	it **was playing**
you **were playing**	we **were playing**
he **was playing**	you **were playing**
she **was playing**	they **were playing**

Subject + ***was / were*** **+ verb in *-ing* form**

Negative	
Full form	**Short form**
I **was not playing**	I **wasn't playing**
you **were not playing**	you **weren't playing**
he **was not playing**	he **wasn't playing**
she **was not playing**	she **wasn't playing**
it **was not playing**	it **wasn't playing**
we **were not playing**	we **weren't playing**
you **were not playing**	you **weren't playing**
they **were not playing**	they **weren't playing**

Subject +	*was not* (*wasn't*) *were not* (*weren't*)	+ verb in *-ing* form

1 We make the affirmative form of the past progressive with the subject + *be* in the simple past (*was / were*) + the main verb in the *-ing* form.
The teacher **was writing** on the whiteboard.

2 We make the negative form of the past progressive with the subject + *be* in the simple past (*was / were*) + *not* + the main verb in the *-ing* form.
The teacher **wasn't writing** on the whiteboard.

3 In spoken and written informal English, we usually use the negative short form.
We **weren't surfing** the Internet.
(= We **were not** surfing the Internet.)

4 We use the past progressive to talk about actions happening at a specific time in the past.
Yesterday evening at seven o'clock, I **was watching** TV.
I **was waiting** for the bus at 4 p.m. this afternoon.

5 We sometimes use time expressions to show the length of time that passed:
- ***from ... to***
  Suki was shopping **from** 3 **to** 4 p.m.
- ***between ... and***
  We were having breakfast **between** 7 **and** 7:30 a.m. this morning.

6 We often use the past progressive to describe a scene, especially when telling a story.
The sun **was shining** and the birds **were singing**.

Past progressive
Interrogative and short answers

Interrogative	
Was I **playing**?	**Was** it **playing**?
Were you **playing**?	**Were** we **playing**?
Was he **playing**?	**Were** you **playing**?
Was she **playing**?	**Were** they **playing**?

Was / Were	+ subject +	verb in *-ing* form

Short answers	
Affirmative	**Negative**
Yes, I was.	No, I wasn't.
Yes, you were.	No, you weren't.
Yes, he was.	No, he wasn't.
Yes, she was.	No, she wasn't.
Yes, it was.	No, it wasn't.
Yes, we were.	No, we weren't.
Yes, you were.	No, you weren't.
Yes, they were.	No, they weren't.

Yes, *No,*	+ subject +	*was / were.* *wasn't / weren't.*

1 We make the interrogative form of the past progressive with *Was / Were* + subject + the main verb in the *-ing* form.
Was she **cooking** dinner?

2 We make short answers of the past progressive with *Yes,* + subject + *was / were* or *No,* + subject + *wasn't / weren't.*
"**Was** she **cooking** dinner?"
"**Yes,** she **was**." / "**No,** she **wasn't**."

while

1 We also use the past progressive to talk about two longer actions happening at the same time.

Dave **was washing** the car while the children **were doing** their homework.

2 We use *while* to connect the two actions happening at the same time.

Yara **was listening** to her MP3 player **while** her younger brother **was painting**.

3 *While* can go between the two actions or at the beginning of the sentence.

The teacher was writing in his notebook **while** the students were reading.

While the teacher was writing in his notebook, the students were reading.

Past progressive and simple past + *when / while*

1 We also use the past progressive to talk about a longer action that happened in the past and that was interrupted by a shorter action.

I **was watching** TV when Mom called me.

Mom called me

Past → Now

I was watching TV

2 We can connect the short and longer actions with *when* or *while*.

The teacher **came** into class **while** we **were making** a lot of noise.

They **were walking** down the street **when** they **saw** an accident.

3 *When* can come before the shorter action in the simple past or longer action in the past progressive.

Jess was running **when** she fell.

When Jess was running, she fell.

4 *While* must always come before the longer action in the past progressive.

While they were playing cards, someone robbed the house.

Word list

Crime

kidnap someone ______________

mug someone ______________

murder someone ______________

pick someone's pocket ______________

rob a bank ______________

shoplift ______________

steal a painting ______________

vandalize a building ______________

Criminals

kidnapper ______________

mugger ______________

murderer ______________

pickpocket ______________

robber ______________

shoplifter ______________

thief ______________

vandal ______________

Student Book pp.74–75, p.77

7 Exercises

Vocabulary

Crime

1 Complete the verbs with the missing letters.

1 k i d n a p
2 s _ _ _ _ _ _ _ _
3 r _ _
4 v _ _ _ _ _ _ _ _ _
5 p _ _ _ _ _ _ _ _ _ _ _ _ _ _ _ _ _ _ _
6 m _ _

2 Change the underlined words with a word from the box.

kidnapped mugger murderer ~~rob~~ pickpocket shoplifter stolen vandalized

The man tried to take money from the bank. rob

1 You're a very clever man, but I know you shot the professor. ______________
2 The woman took three iPods from PC Palace. We found them in her coat. ______________
3 The man showed me a knife and I gave him my wallet. ______________
4 Diane damaged a bus stop. ______________
5 A thief has taken a painting from a museum in Paris. ______________
6 A young man took a wallet from a man's jacket on the train. ______________
7 I have taken your uncle. If you give me $10,000,000, you will see him again. ______________

Grammar

Past progressive
Affirmative and negative

3 Complete the sentences with the correct affirmative or negative form of the past progressive.

Carl and Dan weren't doing (not do) their homework, they were playing (play) table tennis.

1 Lisa ______________ (not sleep), she ______________ (dance).
2 Emily ______________ (not listen) to music, she ______________ (paint).
3 The cat ______________ (not play) with a ball, he ______________ (drink) milk.
4 Dad ______________ (not play) computer games, he ______________ (read).
5 Mom ______________ (not write) an e-mail, she ______________ (watch) TV.

Past progressive
Interrogative and short answers

4 Complete the dialogue with the correct past progressive forms of the verbs.

Officer Were you sitting (you / sit) in a car in East Street from eight thirty to nine o'clock yesterday morning?
Billy Yes, I was.
Officer 1 ______________ (you / talk) with a tall man with dark glasses?
Billy Yes, I 2 ______________. I was with Terry, the driver.
Officer 3 ______________ (you / wait) for someone?
Billy Yes, we 4 ______________. Our friends were in the bank.
Officer 5 ______________ (they / rob) the bank?
Billy Well … yes … they 6 ______________.
Officer And, 7 ______________ (you / wear) a hat?
Billy No, I 8 ______________. It was a theater mask. I'm also an actor.
Officer Good! You'll enjoy the prison theater group.

while

5 Match the sentence halves.

1 Our neighbors are really noisy. While I was trying to sleep last night … *e*
2 I saw you yesterday. You were walking down Launton Street with your mom while … ☐
3 Gary knows about the party. He was listening … ☐
4 I was talking to Mom in the kitchen … ☐
5 It's not fair. My brother was watching TV … ☐
6 John's really impolite. He was sending text messages in the theater … ☐

a I was waiting for a bus with my dad.
b while I was cleaning our room.
c while she was cooking dinner.
d while we were talking about it on the phone.
~~e~~ they were playing loud music.
f while I was acting in the play.

Past progressive and simple past + *when / while*

6 Complete the dialogue with the past progressive forms of the verbs.

Officer Please tell me exactly what you *saw* (see).
Mei Well, I [1] ________ (watch) TV when I [2] ________ (hear) a noise in the street, so I [3] ________ (go) outside. I [4] ________ (stand) in the yard when a man [5] ________ (come) out of the bookstore.
Officer [6] ________ (he / carry) anything?
Mei Yes, there was a big bag and he [7] ________ (have) a gun.
Officer What [8] ________ (happen) next?
Mei I [9] ________ (call) the police, but the man [10] ________ (run) across the park while I [11] ________ (talk) with the officer on the phone.
Officer What [12] ________ (he / wear)?
Mei Black pants and a black shirt.
Officer And what [13] ________ (the man / look) like?
Mei Tall … brown hair … glasses … in fact, he [14] ________ (look) like you!

Round-up

7 Choose the correct answers.

When the police (arrived) / **were arriving** at Danny's house, Danny [1]**work / was working** at his computer. When the police [2]**were arresting / arrested** him, Danny [3]**stole / was stealing** thousands of dollars a month … using the computers in his bedroom.
Danny [4]**learned / was learning** how to hack one summer vacation when he [5]**worked / was working** in a computer store. He [6]**started / was starting** a game with some friends at the store, hacking into their computers. Then one day while Danny [7]**was hacking / hacked** into a bank's website, he [8]**was discovering / discovered** how to get people's credit card numbers.
After that, it was easy to steal money. First, he [9]**downloaded / was downloading** thousands of credit card numbers, then he [10]**was selling / sold** the numbers to criminals. Danny thought he was very intelligent. He was only sixteen years old, but he [11]**made / was making** lots of money. Then the police [12]**were catching / caught** Danny and he [13]**was going / went** to a junior prison for two years. One day while he [14]**was sitting / sat** in the prison, he had a new idea for a computer program – a program to catch hackers! Now Danny works with the police – he's helping them to catch young hackers.

8 Read the text again. Write true sentences.

Danny learned to hack when he was studying ICT.
Danny learned to hack when he was working in a computer store.

1 He discovered how to get people's credit card numbers while he was playing a game.
____
2 Danny sold credit card numbers to banks.
____
3 He was making a lot of money when the police caught him.
____
4 Danny helps the police catch shoplifters.
____

7 Communication

Reporting a crime

1 Complete the dialogue with the phrases in the box.

> ~~can I help you?~~
> it happened at four o'clock this afternoon
> I want to report a crime   ran away   stole
> they were   they were wearing

Officer *Can I help you?*
Ian Yes, [1] ____________.
Officer What happened?
Ian Some boys [2] ____________ my bag.
Officer What were you doing?
Ian I was walking along Redmond Street when two boys stopped me.
Officer What did they do?
Ian One boy pushed me and the other boy stole my bag. Then they [3] ____________.
Officer What time did it happen?
Ian [4] ____________.
Officer What was in the bag?
Ian Some books, my wallet, some money, and my keys.
Officer What did the boys look like?
Ian [5] ____________ fifteen or sixteen. [6] ____________ jeans and jackets.

2 Match the questions and answers.

1 How can I help you? *c*
2 What happened? ☐
3 Where did it happen? ☐
4 What time did it happen? ☐
5 What did he look like? ☐

a At about three thirty.
b He was wearing a sweatshirt and jeans.
~~c~~ I want to report a crime.
d Near the river. A lot of people were watching, but nobody helped the woman.
e A teenager mugged a woman and he stole her bag.

3 You saw a crime and want to report it to the police. Use the information and the picture to complete the conversation.

Crime: Man stole neighbor's computer
Place: Moore Street
Time: ten o'clock in the morning, I was making my bed in my bedroom and looking out of the window

Officer Can I help you?
You [1] ____________
Officer What happened?
You [2] ____________
Officer Where was this?
You [3] ____________
Officer What time was it?
You [4] ____________
Officer What were you doing?
You [5] ____________
Officer What was the man wearing?
You [6] ____________
Officer What about his hair?
You [7] ____________
Officer Thank you for the information. It will be very useful for the investigation.

Student Book p.76

Reading

Take our streets back from the gangs!

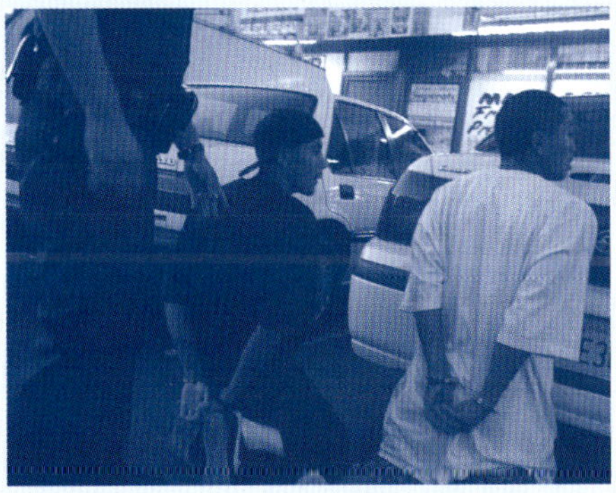

Gang crime is a huge problem in the United States. In Chicago there are over 100 street gangs and about 75,000 gang members. It's the same in other big cities. Some of the biggest gangs like the 18th Street Gang from Los Angeles, even have members in other countries! The gangs sell drugs and carry guns and they fight other gangs. However, people are slowly finding ways to help these young people and to make the streets safer.

1 ____________

Many rap and hip-hop musicians grew up in dangerous neighborhoods and they have friends or family in the street gangs. Now some of them are helping gang members to become musicians instead of criminals. LA street gangs started to record CDs in the 1990s. People in other cities are now following their example.

2 ____________

When the police and parents talk about gang violence, most young people don't want to listen, but when an ex-gang member visits a school it's different. The students listen because the ex-gang members really know what life in a gang is like. Ex-gang members also meet gangs on the street and appear on radio and TV, too.

3 ____________

In some cities gang members can choose to go on an activity vacation at a youth camp. They learn camping skills and make new friends. Youth camps are becoming really popular with gang members because many of them have never left their neighborhoods before. It's a new experience for them and it helps them to think about their lives.

1 **Match the paragraphs with the headings.**

a Visiting Schools
b Gangsta Rap
c Youth Camps

2 **Read the article again. Then answer the questions.**

1 How many gang members live in Chicago?

____

2 What does the writer say about the 18th Street Gang?

____

3 Who started recording music in the 1990s?

____

4 Who do students listen to at schools? Why?

____

5 What do gang members learn on camps?

____

6 Why are youth camps popular with gang members?

____

Writing

3 **Look at the photo. Then answer the questions.**

- What were the people doing when the photo was taken?
- How do gangs use graffiti?
- Is graffiti a problem in your city?

4 **Write a story. Use your ideas from exercise 3.**

The boys were writing graffiti when the police car stopped behind them …

Student Book pp.78–79

8 Grammar rules

Relative pronouns: *who* / *which* / *that*

People
The movie is about an explorer. He finds an island. The movie is about a man **who** / **that** finds an island.

Things
She has a rabbit. It lives in the yard. She has a rabbit **which** / **that** lives in the yard.
This is a bridge. It connects Rio de Janeiro and Niterói in Brazil. This is a bridge **which** / **that** connects Rio de Janeiro and Niterói in Brazil.

1 **Relative clauses give important information about a noun. Relative clauses are introduced by relative pronouns. We use relative pronouns to avoid repeating a name or pronoun.**
Joe's the new student. He started high school last week.
Joe's the new student **who** / **that** started high school last week.
This is my new computer. I bought it from my friend.
This is my new computer **which** / **that** I bought from my friend.

2 **We use the relative pronoun *who* for people.**

He wrote about a scientist **who** built a time machine.

3 **We use the relative pronoun *which* with animals and objects.**
The snakes **which** you have just seen come from South America.
This is the camera **which** Mo Li used to take photos on her vacation.

4 **We use the relative pronoun *that* with people, animals, and objects. We usually use *that* in informal spoken and written English.**
Martin is the man **that** we saw yesterday.
That is the café **that** is open until 10 p.m.

The infinitive of purpose

1 **An infinitive is *to* + the base form of the verb.**

2 **We use an infinitive to express a person's reason for doing something.**
I went to a café **to buy** a sandwich.
NOT ~~I went to a café for buying a sandwich~~.
NOT ~~I went to a café for to buy a sandwich~~.

Which one ...? / Which ones ...?

1 **We use *one* instead of a singular noun.**
a small bottle → a small **one**

2 **We use *ones* instead of a plural noun.**
small bottles → small **ones**

3 **We can use *Which one ...? / Which ones ...?* as object pronouns in the interrogative form to refer to people or objects. We use them:**
- **when the choice is limited.**
"There's some orange juice and some water. **Which one** would you like?"
- **to avoid repetition.**
"Can I have some apples?"
"**Which ones?** The big ones or the small ones?"

Word list

Human achievement – nouns
architect ____________________
artist ____________________
composer ____________________
explorer ____________________
inventor ____________________
politician ____________________
scientist ____________________
writer ____________________

Human achievement – verbs
build ____________________
compose music ____________________
debate ____________________
design ____________________
discover ____________________
draw ____________________
explore ____________________
invent ____________________
negotiate ____________________
paint ____________________
travel ____________________
write ____________________

Student Book pp.82–83, p.85

8 Exercises

Vocabulary

Human achievement

1 Write the names of the professions.

inventor

1 ______________

2 ______________

3 ______________

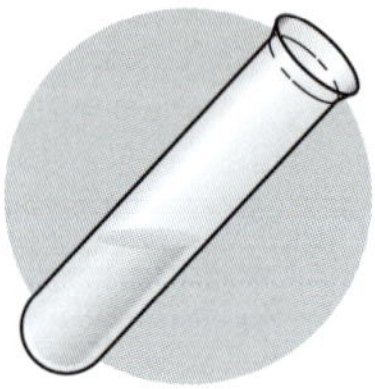

4 ______________

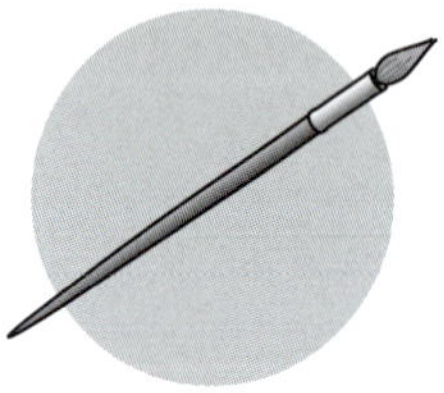

5 ______________

6 ______________

7 ______________

2 Write the professions.

John Cabot sailed to Canada in 1497.
explorer

1 Ian Fleming created the character James Bond.
____

2 Wilhelm Conrad Röntgen discovered X-rays.
____

3 Josephine Cochrane created a mechanical dishwasher in 1886. ______________

4 Frida Kahlo painted in Mexico in the 20th century. ______________

5 Antonio Vivaldi wrote the violin concertos the *Four Seasons*. ______________

6 Abraham Lincoln was president of the U.S. from 1865 to 1869. ______________

Grammar

Relative pronouns: *who / which / that*

3 Choose the correct answers.

Percy Jackson and the Olympians is a series of fantasy stories (**which**) / **who** are famous all over the world.

1 Rick Riordan is the author **which / who** wrote *Percy Jackson and the Olympians* books.

2 The books are about a boy called Percy **which / who** has dyslexia.

3 He discovers he is the son of a Greek god. He goes to Half-Blood Camp – a camp for children **who / which** have one Greek God parent.

4 Percy returns to Half-Blood Camp several times and has adventures **who / that** change his life.

5 Percy meets many people and gods on his adventures **who / which** help him on his way.

6 In 2010, 20th Century Fox made a movie of the first book **who / that** stars Logan Lerman and Alexandra Daddario.

4 Rewrite the sentences with *who* or *which*.

Masaoka Shiki was a Japanese poet. He lived in the 19th century.
Masaoka Shiki was a Japanese poet who lived in the 19th century.

1 *Mona Lisa* is a famous painting. It is in the Louvre Museum in Paris.
____

2 Marco Polo was an Italian explorer. He traveled around Asia in the 13th century.
____

3 The Ford Model T was a car. It was very popular in the 1920s.
____

4 Mark Twain was a writer. He came from the U.S.
____

5 Amelia Earhart was a pilot. She was the first woman to fly solo across the Atlantic Ocean.
____

Infinitive of purpose

5 Max organized a birthday party yesterday. Here is a list of the things he did. Write sentences to explain why he did them.

Things to do:
Get up early – clean the house
Call Luisa and Jun – invite them to the party
Go downtown – buy Isabel a present
Buy some candles – put on the birthday cake
Go to Kevin's house – borrow some CDs
make some ice – put in the drinks
Clean the barbecue – cook the hamburgers

He got up early to clean the house.
1 ______
2 ______
3 ______
4 ______
5 ______
6 ______

Which one ...? / Which ones ...?

6 Which word does *one* / *ones* replace? Read the sentences and circle the correct answers.

There are some (books) on the table. Which ones are yours?
1 Which of those girls is your cousin? The small one.
2 "Put these CDs in the bag over there." "Which one?"
3 The shoes in this store are cool. Which ones do you prefer?
4 "Which of those men is your basketball coach?" "The one with a beard."
5 The songs on this CD are great! Which one is your favorite?
6 This museum has some cool paintings. I like the ones in this room best.

Round-up

7 Complete the text with *who*, *which*, or the infinitive form of the verbs in the box.

change keep say send show stop

Welcome to e-Gifts.com

Are you someone who likes giving gifts? If you're looking for gift ideas [1]______ are fun and different then **e-Gifts.com** is for you!
The **Waterproof MP3 Player Case** is the perfect gift for someone [2]______ wants to listen to music in the bath! It's thick enough [3]______ water out, but it's thin enough [4]______ songs easily!
Price $8.99

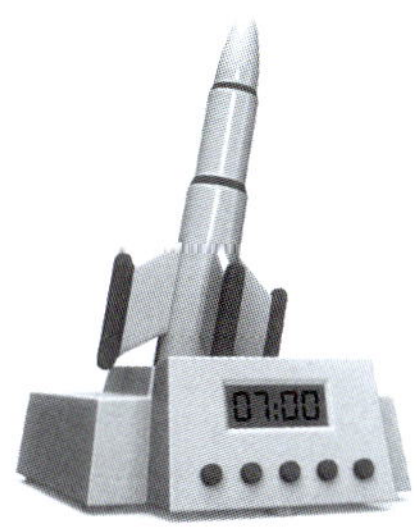

Do you know anyone [5]______ can't get out of bed in the morning? **Rocket Alarm Clock** is the perfect gift for them! First there's a loud alarm. Then there's a countdown "10, 9, 8 ..." Finally a rocket launches across your room! You have to get out of bed and put the rocket back on the base [6]______ the alarm!
Price: $20.50

The **Drivemessenger** is for someone [7]______ spends a lot of time in the car. You use it [8]______ messages to other drivers. Push a button [9]______ "Thanks", "Sorry" or [10]______ a smiley face.
Price: $34

8 Complete the questions with *one* or *ones*. Then answer them.

Which one is the most expensive?
The Rocket Alarm Clock.
1 Which ______ are for children?
2 Which ______ is only for adults?
3 Which ______ is the most unusual?

8 Communication

Discussing what things are for

1 Complete the dialogues with the phrases in the box.

for reading to keep what are these?
what are they for? what's it for?
what's this? ~~what's this gadget?~~

1
A *What's this gadget?*
B It's a book light.
A 1 ________________
B It's 2 ________________ in the dark. You attach it to a book and you use it to read in bed or in the car.

2
A 3 ________________
B It's an external hard drive.
A What's it for?
B It's for storing information from your computer. You use it 4 ________________ back-up copies of your computer files.

3
A 5 ________________
B They're aqua globes.
A 6 ________________
B They're for watering your plants. You put water in them and then you put them in your plant pots.

2 Match the questions and answers.

1 What's this? [a]
2 What's it for? [ ]
3 What are these? [ ]
4 What are they for? [ ]

~~a~~ It's a portable charging station.
b They're for hanging photos on your wall.
c They're photo pockets.
d You use it to charge your cell phone or your MP3 player.

3 Write the two dialogues in the correct order.

It's for translating words.
It's a travel translator. I want one!
They're for keeping your hands warm.
They're hand warmers.
They're useless! I wear gloves when it's cold!
What are they for? What are those?
What's it for? ~~What's that?~~

1
A What's that?
B 1 ________________
A 2 ________________
B 3 ________________
A 4 ________________

2
A 5 ________________
B 6 ________________
A 7 ________________
B 8 ________________
A 9 ________________

4 Write dialogues with the information in the product descriptions.

Product description
Name: MP3 Sunglasses
Use: protect your eyes and listen to music
Price: $80

A What are these?
B 1 ________________
A What are they for?
B 2 ________________
A How much are they?
B 3 ________________

Product description
Name: e-book
Use: read and store digital books
Price: $215

A 4 ________________
B 5 ________________
A 6 ________________
B 7 ________________
A 8 ________________
B 9 ________________

Student Book p.84

Skills

Reading

1 Read the article about Einstein. Match the titles to the paragraphs.

~~Einstein was slow to talk.~~ He didn't like school. He was eccentric.
He became interested in science when he was five years old. He was a talented musician.

THE MANY FACES OF ALBERT EINSTEIN

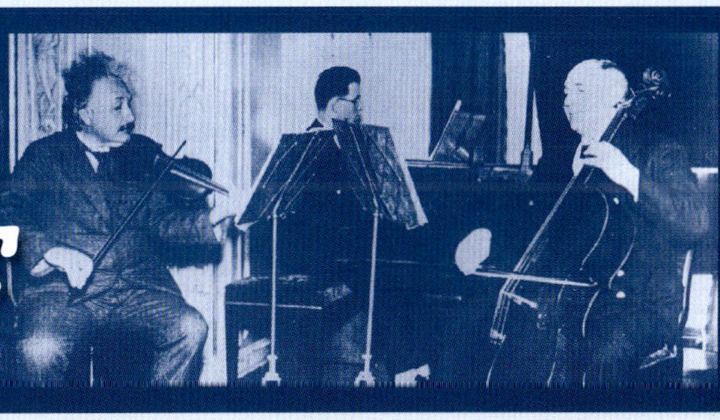

Everybody knows that Albert Einstein was a genius. He was the German-born scientist who developed the theory of relativity. Not many people know, however, that he didn't speak properly until he was nine years old and that he left school without any qualifications!
Here are five fun facts about the world's smartest genius!

1 Einstein was slow to talk.
As a child, Einstein rarely spoke and his parents were worried that he had a problem. He always thought about what he wanted to say very carefully before he said anything. Some people believe this was a sign that he was a great thinker.

2 ______________________
When Einstein was a young child his father gave him an object which changed his life - a compass. Einstein was curious about the fact that the compass always pointed in the same direction and he wanted to understand why.

3 ______________________
Einstein was a good student, but he didn't like school and he left without any qualifications! Later he went to a special school in Switzerland to finish his education. He stayed in Switzerland to attend university and he developed the theory of relativity when he was only 26 years old!

4 ______________________
Einstein loved music and he was an excellent violinist. He used music to help him relax and think more clearly.

5 ______________________
Einstein was also woll known for his eccentric behavior. He didn't cut his hair often and he didn't wear socks, for example. He created the stereotype of the "eccentric scientist"!

2 Read the article again. Then answer the questions.

1 Who was Albert Einstein?
2 Why were Einstein's parents worried when he was a child?
3 What was the object that changed Einstein's life?
4 Why did Einstein go to a special school in Switzerland?
5 What did Einstein use music for?
6 What was Einstein also well-known for?

Writing

3 Write a short biography about an important person of the past. Answer the questions and then write a paragraph about him or her.

- When and where was he / she born?
- What was his / her profession?
- When and why did he / she become famous?
- What other things was he / she famous for?

OXFORD
UNIVERSITY PRESS

Great Clarendon Street, Oxford OX2 6DP

Oxford University Press is a department of the University of Oxford. It furthers the University's objective of excellence in research, scholarship, and education by publishing worldwide in

Oxford New York

Auckland Cape Town Dar es Salaam Hong Kong Karachi Kuala Lumpur Madrid Melbourne Mexico City Nairobi New Delhi Shanghai Taipei Toronto

With offices in

Argentina Austria Brazil Chile Czech Republic France Greece Guatemala Hungary Italy Japan Poland Portugal Singapore South Korea Switzerland Thailand Turkey Ukraine Vietnam

OXFORD and OXFORD ENGLISH are registered trade marks of Oxford University Press in the UK and in certain other countries

First published 2011

2015 2014

10 9 8

ISBN: 978 0 19 446265 5

Printed in China

This book is printed on paper from certified and well-managed sources.

ACKNOWLEDGEMENTS

The authors and publishers would like to thank all the teachers and schools who have given generously of their time and expertise during the development of the course.

Special acknowledgement is due to Claire Thacker for the Curriculum extra lessons, and for the Online Skills Practice material.

Illustrations by: Adrian Barclay pp12, 20; Claude Bordeleau pp4, 66, 74, 77, 82, W23 (ex 6), W28, W29; Paul Daviz pp6, 8, 21, 23, 33, 42, 43, 54, 65, W10, W12, W16, W23 (ex8), W34, W40, W44; Bruno Drummond pp5 (ex 10, ex 14), 11, 22, 46, 47 (ex 7); James Elston pp5 (ex 16), 47 (ex 9), 51; Andy Parker pp84, C1, C5, C6, C8, W47; Alan Rowe pp26, 35, 85, W35 (ex6), W36; Fred Van Deelen pp14, 19, W48, W22; Peters and Zabransky pp10, 38, C7, W25, W45, W46.

The publisher would like to thank the following for their permission to reproduce photographs: Alamy Images pp7 (Charlie Chaplin/Photos 12), 10 (ghost town, California/Interfoto), 10 (Calico ghost town/Ian Dagnall), 16 (woman on laptop/David J. Green), 17 (motorbike/Brad Van Gyzen/BSV Photography), 17 (female driver/Stephen Oliver), 18 ('How Clean is Your House'/Jack Carey), 18 (dirty dishes/foodfolio), 18 (cloths/Tig Photo), 18 (washing up/Andrew Paterson), 19 (cleaning sink/Jochen Tack), 19 (cleaning/vario images GmbH & Co.KG), 27 (paperboy/brt Photo), 28 (New York City/Keith Levit), 30 (graduates/Ellen Isaacs), 30 (Wedding reception tables/Atlaspix), 32 (mother & daughter/Bubbles Photolibrary), 38 (rainforest/David Noton Photography), 44 (chimneys/Paul Glendell), 44 (factory pollution/Jon Bower Pollution), 48 (Seattle/Craig Steven Thrasher), 52 (three zorbs/Purestock), 52 (man inside zorb/Bill Bachmann), 63 (Vancouver/John Elk III), 64 (souvenir t-shirt/D.Hurst), 64 (coffee/Photostock-Dieter Heinemann), 64 (caps/Michael Matthews), 69 (Central Park/Janusz Gniadek), 69 (Broadway adverts/Martin Bond), 70 (bear/imagebroker), 70 (Skagway, Alaska/Ron Niebrugge), 86 (John Logie Baird/Pictorial Press Ltd), 86 (old CRT TV/Tony Cordoza), 86 (watching TV/R1), 87 (plasma TV/Judith Collins), 87 (girl with mobile/Datacraft-Sozaijiten), 87 (Apple iPhone/Cuboimages srl), 87 (solar backpack/Richard Levine), C1 (washing machine/mediablitzimages (UK) Limited), C1 (eco cleaning products/Michael Willis), C1 (eco-cleaners/Michael Willis), C3 (big bang/Ace Stock Limited), C5 (Homer bust/Mary Evans Picture Library), W7 (Amish Children/H Mark Weidman Photography, Amish horse & cart/Andre Jenny), W7 (Amish school bus/Dennis Macdonald), W11 (girl with puppy/Jeff Greenberg), W19 (children gardening/David Grossman), W19 (Pine Ridge/L. Zacharie), W29 (Bear Grylls/Barrie Neil), W48 (electronic dictionary/Oleksiy Maksymenko Photography), W48 (hand warmers/Phil Degginger), W49 (Albert Einstein/Interfoto), W49 (compass/Terry Matthews), W49 (Einstein plays violin/Mary Evans Picture Library); Corbis pp30 (trapeze/Fabrice Vallon/Sygma), 44 (polar bear/Richard Wear/Design Pics), W13 (Girls Washing Clothes/Underwood & Underwood), W41 (computer hacker/Comstock); Getty Images pp17 (cyclist/Aaron Farley/Riser), 17 (man crossing/Brick House Pictures/Iconica), 24 (volleyball/Chris Salvo/Taxi), 52 (pushing zorb/Bernhard Limberger/Look), 56 (bowling/Dennis O'Clair/Stone), 58 (family/Andersen Ross/Iconica), 58 (scuba/Philippe Poulet/Taxi), 59 (friends/Leon/Riser), 69 (Metropolitan Museum of Art, New York/Bloomberg via Getty Images), 70 (Alaska/Chip Porter/The Image Bank), 80 (Tim Berners-Lee/Dani Pozo/AFP), 80 ((CERN) scientists/Fabrice Coffrini/AFP), W13 (Kitchen maids/Hulton Deutsch), W31 (Teenagers in desert/Ken Chemus/Taxi), W43 (arrest/Robert Nickelserg), W43 (creating graffiti/Oleg Romanov/Pressphotos), W43 (music teacher/Susana Gonzalez/Bloomberg), W48 (mp3 sunglasses Vladimir Rys/Bongarts), W48 (e-book readers/Daniel Acker/Bloomberg); iStockphoto pp60 (girl reading/Krystian Kaczmarski), 60 (boy reading/Jaimie Duplass); Kobal Collection pp78 (Holmes profile/20TH Century Fox), 78 (Holmes and Watson/Hammer), W37 (jetpack/DANJAQ/EON/UA), W37 (Daniel Craig/MGM/United Artists/Sony), W46 (Percy Jackson & The Olympians: The Lightning Thief/Fox 2000 Pictures); OUP pp9 (female student/Comstock), 16 (teens by lockers/Digital Vision), 28 (Statue of Liberty/Photodisc), 31 (smiling woman/Corbis), 32 (businesswoman/Image Source), 44 (traffic jam/Corbis), 53 (students/Somos), 68 (London Eye/Digital Vision), 87 (laptop/David Cook), 87 (backpack/Dennis Kitchen Studio, Inc.), 89 (teen girl/Design Pics); PA Photos: W25 (twister/Wayne Hanna/AP); Photolibrary pp19 (maid/Uppercut Images), 31 (smiling woman/Blend Images RF), 31 (Young man smiling/PhotoAlto), 32 (woman with palm-top/Blend Images RF), 32 (computer lesson/Corbis), 34 (teens with laptops/Corbis), C1 (oven cleaning/Digital Vision); PunchStock pp (Teenage girl/Photodisc), 19 (woman dusting/moodboard), 32 (architect/Tetra), 32 (lazy teen/Corbis), 64 (snow globe/Corbis), 87 (notebook/Photodisc), W31 (camping/Brand X Pictures); Reuters Pictures p48 (summer hail storm/Andrew Sheargold); Rex Features pp24 (teen with remote/Carson Ganci/Design Pics Inc), 90 (Wesley Autrey/Sipa Press); Shutterstock pp C3 (north sky star constellation/Zlatko Guzmic), C3 (south sky star constellation/Zlatko Guzmic).

Cover photograph by: Getty (Photodisc)